Sewing LAMPSHADES

Dedication

This book is dedicated to all those who have yearned to be able to create the beautiful lampshades of their imagination. I hope you take these ideas and make them your own.

Sewing LAMPSHADES

Joanna Heptinstall

SEARCH PRESS

Acknowledgements

This book was made possible by the faith of the commissioning editor at Search Press, Katie French; the vision, talent (and endless patience) of senior editor Becky Robbins; confidence to play with fabric instilled in me from the beginning by my wonderful mum Sue Taylor, who also produced the beautiful machine-embroidered design on page 62; my creative and inspiring aunt Bobbie Walkington's invaluable lessons in colour; and the respect for technical skill and unfailing can-do attitude of my grandmother Doris Deighton. Special thanks also to my family and friends for all their support, and especially my husband Simon, and Harry and Millie, for giving me the time and space to do it. Thank you.

First published in 2018

Search Press Limited
Wellwood, North Farm Road,
Tunbridge Wells, Kent TN2 3DR

Text copyright © Joanna Heptinstall 2018
Photographs by Roddy Paine Photographic Studios
Photographs, illustrations and design copyright
© Search Press Limited 2018

ISBN: 978-1-78221-449-6

Suppliers
For details of suppliers, please visit the Search Press website:
www.searchpress.com or Joanna's website:
www.traditionalupholsteryschool.co.uk

Printed in China through Asia Pacific Offset

Contents

Introduction

One day I spotted a tattered lampshade in a junk shop. The fabric was frayed, the fringes dangling and the seams falling apart. Somehow that sad old shade inspired me. I realized that a beautiful lampshade can be like the crown jewels of soft furnishings, the most glorious hand-made feature anyone can add to a room. And I was determined to revive this ailing specimen if I could.

So I took it home and spent hours working out how to re-cover it. Back then there were no handy DIY books. No-one seemed to remember how it was done. Luckily I was already a trained upholsterer… and after practising on dozens of lampshade frames, and trawling a few ancient and wordy textbooks, I worked out some of the basic principles.

Now, many years later, I still absolutely love restoring lampshades. From reviving vintage pleated empire shades with silk chiffon to showing off fabulous modern fabrics on a tailored shade, every single one is a joy. For anyone who loves expressing their own unique style with fabric, lampshade making is an incredibly rewarding craft.

I've designed this collection of projects to teach the core skills of lampshade making and show off how flexible you can be with different fabrics, frames and trimmings. You'll be able to build up your skills as you work through the book, moving from tailored to pleated shades. Some of these ideas were hard won after much trial and error but I'm delighted to be able to pass them on. This book should enable you to make them your own and I hope you'll end up using the skills to express your own creativity in the lovely world of lampshades.

SEWING KIT

If you already sew, then you will have everything you need to start making lampshades already. A domestic sewing machine is essential, along with the usual haberdashery kit: scissors, pins, needles and threads. The list below details some of the lampshade maker's most useful kit.

FABRIC MARKERS

These are essential for accurately marking seams, but must be fully removable to avoid permanent unsightly marks. Tailor's chalks are now available in pen form, giving a more accurate fine line than the traditional triangular block. Water and air-soluble pens are also very useful, and you'll need a soft pencil for making your patterns.

PINS

You will need lots! Choose short pins (approximately 35mm/1½in long) with a glass or plastic head. Short pins are less easily bent and you are not so likely to tangle threads around them when stitching, and beaded heads are kinder to fingertips. Bear in mind that over the course of making a lampshade, many pins are likely to bend, so buy economically.

If you are working with silk and other delicate fabrics, invest in fine silk pins, which are less likely to make holes in your delicate fabrics.

Traditionally 'lill' pins, very short craft pins, were used, but they can be fiddly and their tiny steel heads can quickly make fingertips sore – something to aspire to once you have mastered the techniques.

NEEDLES AND THREADS

You will need a selection of fine needles for hand sewing, and you will also find a small, fine curved needle useful when attaching trims to shades. Hand sewing is best done with an extra-strong or upholstery-weight thread, rather than a standard weight. Thicker thread is easier to work with, and less likely to snap and tangle. When hand sewing, a thimble is useful to push the needle through many layers. Alternatively, bind your 'needle-pushing' finger in plaster strapping to save sore fingers.

MEASURING TOOLS

A soft haberdashery tape measure is vital for accurately measuring around the curves of lampshades. You will also find a long straight clear plastic ruler useful when marking up fabric for pleated shades and for making handmade trimmings.

GLUE

Traditionally, fabric was always stitched to the lampshade frame, but the advent of affordable, easy-to-work-with and long-lasting glues has opened up a quicker alternative method to lampshade makers. The ideal glue is viscous rather than runny, as it should not bleed into the fabric. It must hold fast in a short time, be long-lasting and not 'yellow' over time. Of course, if you prefer, you need not use any glue at all. Lampshade stitch is described on page 31.

SCISSORS

You will need a pair of sharp fabric-cutting scissors, plus a smaller pair for snipping threads and getting into tight corners. To keep your fabric scissors sharper for longer, you will also need a pair of sturdy general scissors to strip old fabric from frames and to cut out paper templates.

BINDING TAPE

Binding a wire frame makes it possible to pin and sew fabric to it. Traditionally, a loosely woven cotton tape, with selvedge along both edges, was used. Often called cotton India tape, it is available in white, unbleached and black. It comes in various widths: 10mm (½in) is the most useful standard width. For tiny shades you may need narrower 7mm (¼in) tape to prevent bulky binding. It is always more economical to buy tape on a roll, rather than cut lengths.

WRAPPING AND STORING

Lampshades don't thrive if crushed, overly handled or allowed to get dusty. With this in mind, store your in-progress shades carefully by wrapping in soft cellophane, cotton muslin or even a clean pillowcase. Alternatively, hanging them from a hook on the sewing-room ceiling will keep them well out of harm's way while you are not working on them.

FABRICS

Traditionally, silk has always been the lampshade maker's choice. Its natural sheen is shown off perfectly when stretched across a rounded surface. Closely woven silk threads diffuse light perfectly, like stained glass. Silk is durable and naturally heat-resistant. It is available in many colours, weights and finishes. It can also be relatively inexpensive. These are all qualities that lampshade makers should look for in their choice of fabrics, silk or otherwise, as today the fun is in enjoying the creative freedom of the fabulous prints, weaves and textures available to us. Here's a quick guide:

PRINTS

Checks, stripes, spots, florals, huge prints, teeny prints, vintage prints… the choice is vast. It makes sense to choose a small-scale print for a small shade and a larger one for a large shade, but why not play with creative drama and work with a massive-scale pattern? Take care when choosing evenly spaced small motifs as these can become obvious rows when working across a curved surface. Lampshades provide a wonderful opportunity to show off treasured scraps of vintage fabrics, but check first that the fibres are still strong enough to be pulled taut and that there are no tiny moth holes that will become obvious when lit.

WOOLS AND THICK TEXTURES

Wools, tweeds, velvets… surely a no-go for lampshade makers? Not necessarily. A thick wool cloth will give out a subdued light but is covered with a gentle halo of tiny wool fibres, which diffuse light well and create a cosy feel. Velvet allows very little light through, perhaps just pinpricks, but a velvet-covered shade will allow light out of the top and bottom, creating drama in a dark space. Teamed with a strong-coloured lining, these fabrics can be a huge success.

SILK

Always a successful choice, silk has many weights, textures and colours to enjoy. Silk dupion is one of the most affordable and versatile silk fabrics, working well for fitted covers and linings, and making superbly crisp pleats too. Alternatively, light, floppy silk chiffon is tricky to handle but utterly gorgeous when folded as it is tissue-paper thin. As it is light enough to hold its own weight, it makes wonderful ruched and gathered trimmings (see page 102).

COTTON AND LINEN

Like silk, these fibres are naturally heat-resistant. The finer the weave, the better the light will diffuse through the shade. Patchwork-weight cottons work well, as light diffuses successfully through the closely woven fine threads. Light shining through a heavy slubby linen, however, will look grainy, so this works best when teamed with a fine lining such as habotai silk.

TRIMMINGS

Fringes, tassels, gimp braids, ribbons… these are the icing on the cake for lampshade makers. The scale and size of a trimming has a huge effect on the finished look of a lampshade, often changing the whole shape and proportion. There is a wide choice of ready-made trimmings available, designed for craft and soft furnishing use. Take time to order samples. It is always worthwhile to choose trimmings at the same time as your fabric, rather than trying to find the perfect match afterwards.

SAFETY

Natural fabrics such as cotton, linen and silk are naturally flame-retardant and unlikely to scorch or burn when used with a modern 60-watt (or less) bulb. However, it is important to treat all fabrics with flame-retardant spray prior to use. These sprays can be bought from haberdashery and hardware shops. Always follow the instructions and work in a well-ventilated space. Do carry out a test patch first, as some fabric colours may run when sprayed.

It is recommended that a 60-watt bulb, or less, is used with a fabric shade and fabric should never be closer than 10cm (4in) from the bulb.

All light fittings should be professionally tested before resale. This can be done very cheaply by a local electrician.

KNOW YOUR LAMPSHADE FRAMES

Lampshade frames come in a huge range of shapes and sizes, but they all share the same essential structure. Modern shades are usually plastic-coated to make then rust-proof, but many secondhand ones, and a few modern ones, are a simple bare metal frame.

ELEMENTS OF A LAMPSHADE FRAME

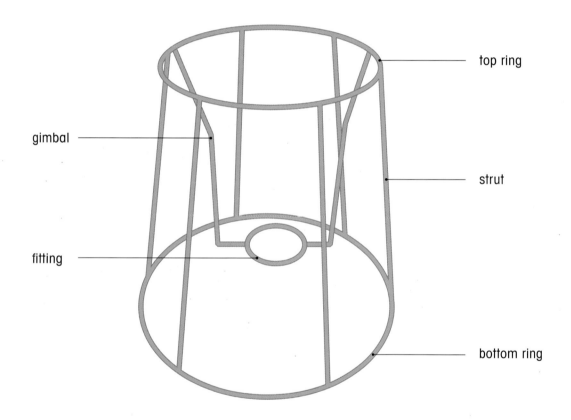

gimbal

top ring

strut

fitting

bottom ring

Top and bottom rings
These are always referred to as rings, even if they are not circular.

Struts
The vertical struts that join the top and bottom rings; they can be straight or curved.

Fitting
This is the part that slots onto the bulb holder of the lamp stand.

Gimbal
Joins the fitting onto the frame, and is usually connected to the top ring unless on a very tall shade. There can be two, three or four gimbals, depending on the size of the frame.

VARIATIONS OF FITTINGS

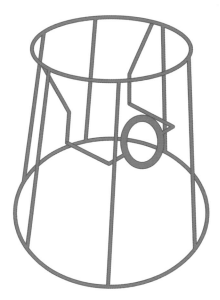

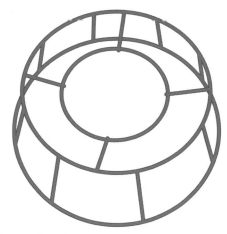

Duplex fitting

A shade with a duplex fitting requires a shade carrier (see below) to fit to a stand, or spider fitting (see below) to fit to a pendant bulb. Duplex fittings tend to be found on larger frames.

Reversible gimbals

A reversible gimbal has a join along the length allowing the fitting to pivot so the shade can be used on a table lamp or pendant lamp. It also allows the shade to be displayed cocked at an angle.

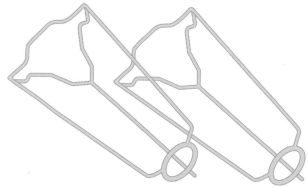

Shade carrier

Shade carriers are available in different heights, from 10cm (4in) to about 25.5cm (10in). This allows the shade to be held on the base at varying heights, making it an incredibly useful and versatile fitting.

Clip fitting

Clip fittings are generally found on smaller shades. The clip fits over the bulb, so care must be taken that the clip doesn't slip and the fabric touch the bulb.

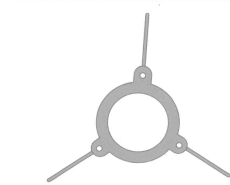

Spider fitting

This allows a duplex fitting (see above) to be attached to a pendant light.

FRAME SHAPES

There is a huge variety of frame shapes available, with many lending themselves to particular covering techniques. Straight-sided shades lend themselves well to knife pleats, while those with a nipped-in empire waistline are designed to show off swathed pleats and gathers. Here is a selection of some of the most common shapes.

Bowed drum

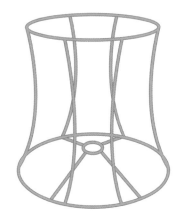

Straight empire

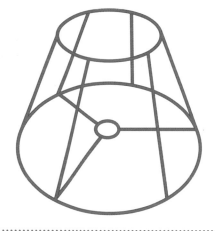

Scalloped empire

Bowed empire with clover bottom ring

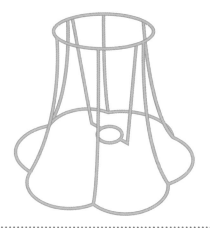

Bowed empire

Banded double scalloped empire

Cone

Dome

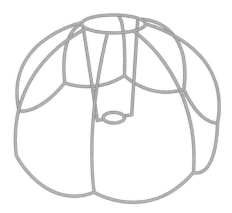

French bell

Inverted Tiffany

Oriental

Square

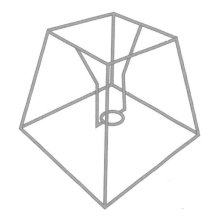

Straight drum

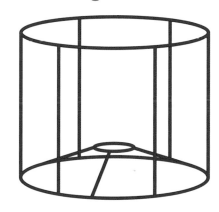

Straight empire
with collar

Tall bowed empire

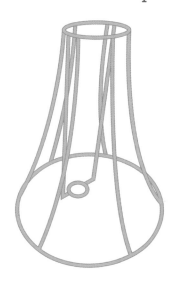

LAMPSHADES OF VERY DIFFERENT SHAPES

When starting out making fitted covers for lampshades, the first decision is how many seams your finished cover should have.

Having the fewest seams – just two – has many advantages. For example, fabric is most likely to wrinkle and pucker near a seam, so the fewer seams you have the better. And with fewer seams, the fabric will flow uninterrupted around the shade, allowing the pattern to be shown off at its best. However, even cut out on the bias, when fabric is at its most stretchy, there is only so much curve you can expect a flat piece of fabric to ease itself around.

If you are not quite sure how many seams you will need, make two templates: one for just two seams (covering half the shade), and another for four seams (covering a quarter of an eight-panelled shade frame). You are likely to be able to tell just by making the template which will work best but, if unsure, make a version of each using scrap fabric and try fitting them on the shade. The one that fits best is the template you should work with. With a little experience, you will be able to gauge this just by looking at the shade.

On very curvaceous shades, such as this scalloped shade, you may need four panels of fabric for your fitted cover, joined by four seams, so each piece of fabric is only covering a quarter of the shade frame.

This tall banded bowed empire shade has very little curve from top to bottom and was successfully covered with just two panels of fabric joined by two seams.

Tailored projects

MAKING A TAILORED SHADE

THE CORE SKILLS

This chapter walks you step by step through the skills required to re-cover a tailored lampshade from scratch. Essentially, you will be stretching a bias-cut fabric cover taut over the frame and securing it in place. You will use this technique for re-covering almost every style of tailored shade.

PREPARING THE FRAME

▶ **1** Your shade frame should be in good condition before you start. Check it is sound and symmetrical, as a distorted frame can cause problems when fitting a tailored cover. Often, a gentle squeeze can pull a slightly bent frame back into shape. Strip off old fabric from vintage frames and peel away glue to leave a smooth clean surface. Take care not to pull any struts out of shape. Rusty frames should be sanded and primed to prevent rust stains seeping through over time.

You will need

» A bowed empire shade frame
» Cotton India tape
» Old sheeting
» Top fabric (patchworking cotton or lightweight linen are ideal)
» Cotton jersey lining fabric
» Tassel trimming
» Braid or ribbon
» Quick-dry, clear all-purpose glue
» Bead-headed pins
» Sewing kit

A selection of tools and materials needed for covering a shade frame.

BINDING THE FRAME

Lampshade frames need to be bound with a woven cotton tape to provide a surface to which you can pin and sew your fabric. Successful binding must be smooth, even and very tight. Loose binding will twist around the frame and allow the fabric to slip; the resulting cover will be baggy and loose, rather than beautifully taut.

Which parts of the frame do I bind?

The top and bottom rings must be bound, as this is where you will pin and sew. In order to make a template, you will also need to bind two of the vertical struts. Which ones – whether adjacent or opposite, for example – will depend on how many seams you need to create for the full cover (see page 16 for guidance).

How much tape do I cut?

You will use approximately three times more tape than the length of the wire strut or ring you are to bind. This will vary according to your style of binding and the thickness of the wire. If the circumference of the ring is very long, you may find it easier to work with pieces cut to the length of your arm, as a very long strip tends to get tangled in the frame as you work.

▶ **2** You will start by binding the two rings – top and bottom. Place one end of the tape diagonally behind a strut and the ring, as shown.

▶ **3** Bring the long end over the ring and down behind to the left of the strut.

▶ **4** Now bring the long end diagonally across the front towards the right.

▶ **5** Working to the right, bind the ring with tape. Aim to bind on the same diagonal slant throughout. The tape should overlap each time by about half. It should lie flat with no wrinkles. As you bind, pull the tape tightly and keep it taut while you loop the tape over the ring by holding it down with the thumb or forefinger of your other hand.

TIP: To check that your binding is tight enough, pinch it between finger and thumb and try to wiggle it. It shouldn't move at all. If it does, it's too loose and must be re-bound.

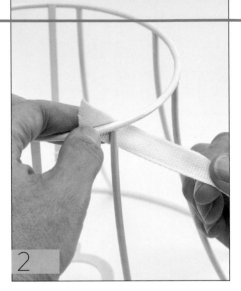

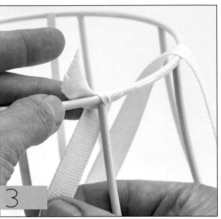

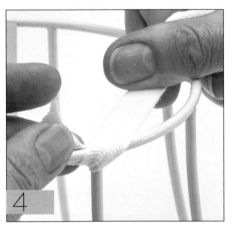

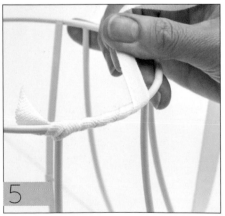

6A

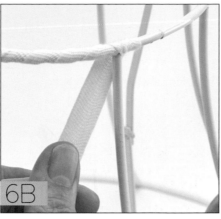
6B

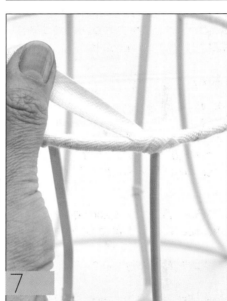
6C

▶ **6** When you reach a strut, work round it by either doing a figure of eight with the tape (as shown in steps 6a–c), which works well on a larger shade frame, or simply by angling the tape so that you avoid wrinkles, which is a better solution for smaller frames.

▶ **7** To finish off when you get back to the start, tuck the long end back under the last loop and pull tight to create a flat knot. Secure with a few stitches in white thread. Repeat for the bottom ring.

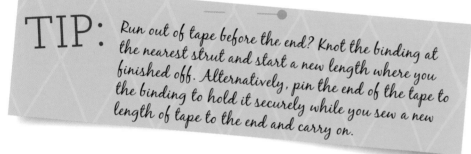

TIP: Run out of tape before the end? Knot the binding at the nearest strut and start a new length where you finished off. Alternatively, pin the end of the tape to the binding to hold it securely while you sew a new length of tape to the end and carry on.

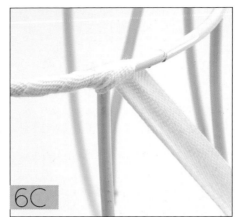
7

MAKING A TEMPLATE

The lining and the main cover for this particular shade are made in two halves, with two seams opposite each other. Not all shade frames can be fitted with a tailored cover using only two seams – see page 16 to work out how many seams you will need to make to cover your shade frame successfully. However many seams you have, the method is the same.

▶ **8** To make the template, start by binding two opposite vertical struts. It doesn't matter which, as the binding will be removed before you fit the lining and top cover. To bind, start with a knot at the top, bind as for the rings, and end with a knot, leaving the tail long so that it can be easily undone.

8

9 Take a piece of old sheeting or calico fabric. Both are non-stretchy, evenly woven but have some 'give' on the bias. To calculate the size of the piece roughly, measure from the top of the left-hand strut around to the bottom of the right hand strut. Add about 5–10cm (2–4in) to this – this gives you the rough height and width to cut.

10 Place your shade frame in front of you with the top ring facing you and the two bound struts at either side. Position the piece of calico over the shade frame at a 45˚ angle, so that the fabric is on the bias. Place a pin centre top, bottom and both sides. At this stage the fabric will look loose and floppy, but don't worry. Remove the pin on the bottom ring, pull the fabric a little tauter and re-pin. Now working from this centre pin on the bottom ring, start pinning from the centre out towards the left-hand strut, pulling the fabric with even tautness. The pins should be about 2cm ($^{13}/_{16}$in) apart. Once done, work from the centre pin out towards the right-hand strut. Turn the shade frame around and do the same around the top ring. At this stage the fabric is still likely to look a little wrinkled, but don't worry – you haven't finished yet! Start at the centre of one of the vertical struts at the side and, working from the centre pin outwards, pin the fabric to the strut, pulling the fabric with the same even tautness. Work both sides the same.

11 Once all the pins are in place, stand back and have a look. You want a uniformly taut skin of fabric over the frame, with no wrinkles or puckers. On close examination, the grain of the fabric should run smoothly, with no dragging or veering off in one direction. To remove any wrinkles, follow the grain of the fabric from the wrinkle to the edge, pull tauter and re-pin.

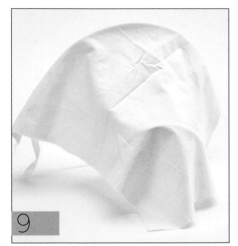

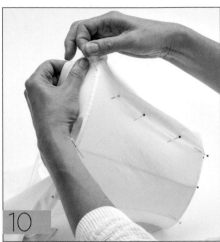

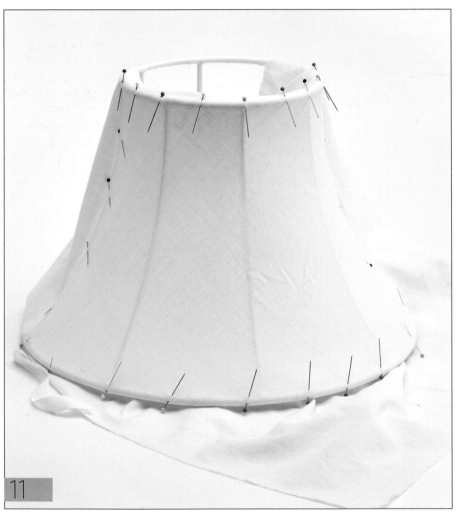

Note the position of the pins, which act like tent pegs, bracing against the strain of the fabric and less likely to prick you as you work.

12 Using a soft pencil, mark around the template, following the line of the wire frame, along the rings and the side struts. Once done, take out all the pins, remove from the frame and cut out, following the pencil line.

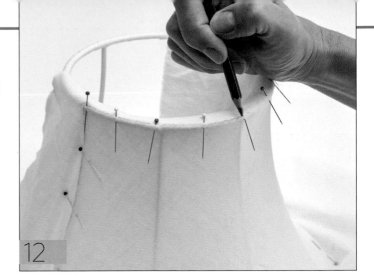

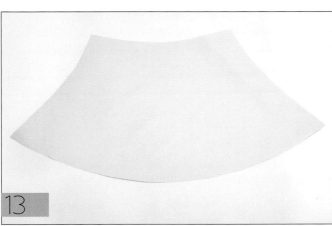

13 It is a good idea to check now that your template is symmetrical. To check, simply fold your template in half: the two seam lines should sit over each other exactly. If they do not, it is likely that your pulling tension was not even. If your template is very out of shape, have another go rather than trying to make do, as working with a wonky template is not going to be successful. If, however, the difference is fairly minor, see the troubleshooting box, below. Once you are happy with your template, unbind the two vertical struts.

For a drum empire shade, your template should now look something like this.

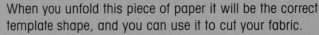

TROUBLESHOOTING

When your template isn't symmetrical

1 Fold your template in half and line up as best you can (pin together if you prefer). Draw a pencil line in between the two sides, finding the average line between the two.

2 Without unfolding, cut along this new line. Place the folded and newly-trimmed template on the fold line of a folded sheet of paper. Draw around it and cut out.

When you unfold this piece of paper it will be the correct template shape, and you can use it to cut your fabric.

Note that not all shade frames can be fitted with a tailored cover using only two seams. See page 16 to work out how many seams you will need to cover your shade frame successfully. However many seams you have, the method is the same.

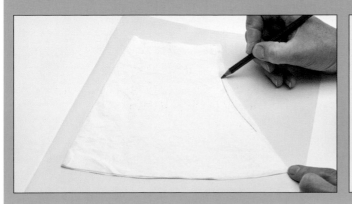

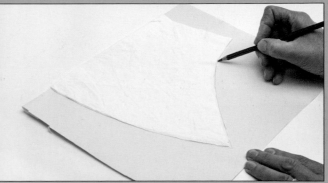

CUTTING OUT THE TOP FABRIC

The same template is used for cutting out both the top fabric and the lining. The top fabric is almost always cut on the bias. This allows the fabric the most 'give' as it eases around the curvy shape of the shade.

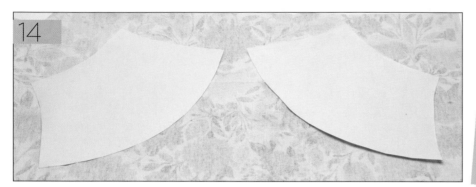

▶ **14** Press your fabric then lay wrong side up on your cutting surface. You should still be able to see any woven or printed pattern. Position your template at 45° to the grain of the fabric, allowing about 1.5cm (⅝in) seam allowance at the side seams and 6–10cm (2½–4in) extra at the top and bottom for handling. The two halves should be cut out at opposite angles, as shown. This is important for patterned or grainy fabrics, which look best on the seams if pattern or texture meet at opposing angles.

▶ **15** Mark the side seams using a removable fabric marker pen or tacking/basting stitches. Indicate the top edge of the template with a mark or tailor's tack (see opposite). Do not mark the top or bottom edges. If your fabric is heavily patterned and you are keen to match the position of the pattern on the shade exactly, then mark out both pieces, as described. Otherwise, you only need to mark up one piece in this way. Cut out the two pieces leaving a 1.5cm (⅝in) allowance at the sides and 6–10cm (2½–4in) at the top and bottom edges.

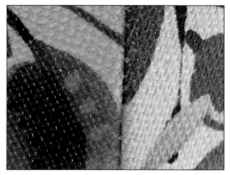

Fabric grain creating a 'V' shape at the seam where the opposing angles of the fabric meet.

SEWING THE TOP FABRIC

▶ **16** Place the two pieces together and pin along the marked side seams, positioning the pins at 90° to the fabric edge. If you have marked both fabric pieces, then these lines must tally exactly. Similarly, ensure that the markers at the top of each seam are in the same place. If you have one, fit your sewing machine with a walking foot to help ease both layers through equally.

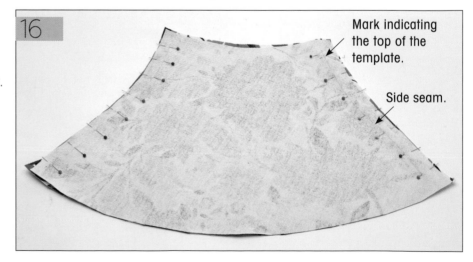

Mark indicating the top of the template.

Side seam.

17 Thread your machine with a matching thread and use a needle appropriate to the weight of your fabric; a blunt or too-large needle may pucker an unforgiving fabric such as silk. Set to a fairly small stitch length, because long stitches may gape open once the fabric is stretched taut. Sew along the line, flowing in from the edge of the fabric, not the start of the marked line – this helps to ease stretch into this sewn line as you work. Then sew a second line, just 2mm (1/16in) to the outside of the first. This double line helps give extra strength to the seam. Sewing the lines side-by-side rather than directly on top of each other helps keep the seams soft and stretchy. When sewing, do not 'lock off' the stitching by going back and forth. After sewing, run the seam between finger and thumb to ease more stretch into the seam.

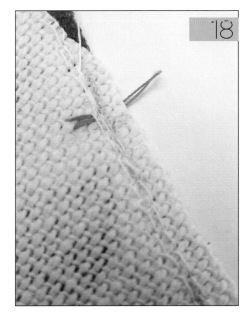

MAKING A TAILOR'S TACK

A tailor's tack is a single overstitch made with needle and contrasting thread to mark a point on a seam. I usually stitch one on each side seam, indicating the top edge of the template shape. This allows me to pin the pieces together accurately. When left in for the fitting stage, they make it easier to line up the top edge of the sewn cover exactly to the top ring of the frame.

Thread a needle with contrasting thread; do not knot it. Using the thread doubled, take a small stitch and pull through to leave a thread end of 1.5–3cm (1/2–1in). Now make a second stitch on top of the first and pull through. Trim off the other end to leave a 1.5–3cm (1/2–1in) thread end. Some people prefer to make a second stitch at right angles to the first, or just take a single stitch.

18 Trim the excess seam allowance to 3mm (1/8in) from the outer stitch line. Make your cutting line neat and sharp, as raggedy edges will be visible when the shade is lit.

FITTING THE OUTER COVER

Work on a clean work surface and have plenty of bead-headed pins to hand.

19 With your frame standing the right way up, pull the top cover over the frame, lining up the seams with two of the vertical struts. Line up the two top markers of the side seams with the top ring.

20 Pin through the fabric and binding to the outside of the frame, with the pin facing downwards, and push all the way down. Once the two seams are pinned, place a pin at the top of each vertical strut. Turn the shade frame over. Take hold of the fabric at one of the side seams and pull, easing some (but not too much) tautness into the fabric. Pin at the bottom ring. Repeat at the other side seam. Continue around the bottom ring, pinning the fabric to the ring at the struts.

At this point you will start to see your lampshade forming. Your fabric shouldn't be baggy if you have pinned with a little tension. Don't worry if it has lots of ripples and looks as if it is not going to fit – this is usual at this stage.

▶ **21** Turn your frame back the right way up so it is standing on the bottom ring. Now fit pins around the top ring, ensuring the fabric is evenly spaced. You should not be hitching the fabric up, but ensuring that it sits in line with the markers at the top of the side seams. The pins should be about 2cm ($^{13}/_{16}$ in) apart – even less on a very small shade.

▶ **22** Now you can turn your frame over again and work more tension into the cover, pinning and stretching until the cover is taut and smooth. This should be done systematically to create an even tension. Start by pulling tension into the side seams and re-pinning. The turn the shade frame around 180° and pull the same amount of tension into the cover at these two points, and re-pin.

▶ **23** Turn again, this time to the points halfway between the four you have already tightened. At this stage eight equally spaced points will be been tightened around the bottom ring of the shade and you should start seeing some real difference to the fit. Now pin between each of these eight points, about 2cm ($^{13}/_{16}$ in) apart, pulling the same tension into the fabric cover.

▶ **24** Look inside the frame and check that the side seams are lying neatly alongside a vertical strut. The raw edge of one seam should be sitting along one side of the strut and, on the opposite side, the seam should be running along the opposite side of the strut.

TROUBLESHOOTING

How taut is correct?
The fabric should be taut enough that, when pressed with the tip of a finger, it resists the push and does not buckle or dent.

Seams aren't lined up straight against the struts?
From the point where the seam bows out away from the strut, follow the grain of the fabric down to the bottom ring. Remove the pin here and pull: you should find that the seam pulls in towards the strut. It may help to remove the pins on the other side of the seam to allow movement.

I still have one or two ripples in the fabric even though it is otherwise very taut. What shall I do?
To get rid of a ripple, follow the grain of the fabric down from that ripple to the bottom ring. At this point re-pin, tightening the fabric. That should immediately smooth away the ripple.

GLUING OR STITCHING?

Traditionally, lampshades were always hand-stitched to the frames. This made them very beautiful pieces of handcrafted work, but also very time-consuming to achieve. Happily, with many effective, quick-drying and affordable glues now available, we have a speedier alternative. While not suitable for every shade or fabric, I would certainly recommend glue as a good solution for most tailored lampshade making. It can, indeed, give better and more polished results than some hand stitchery. For the alternative, lampshade stitch is shown below.

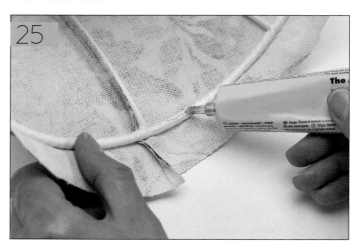

25 Lay your shade down with one of the rings facing you so that you can see inside the shade. Have plenty of bead-headed pins and an old rag to hand. Take a tube of glue or your glue gun and run a thin, even line of glue along the inner edge of the bound ring, from one strut to the next.

26 Wrap the top fabric over the glued surface and, removing and repositioning just one pin at a time so as not to lose tension, pin into place though the glued surface, making sure the pin is pushed through all layers. The pins will now face in towards the middle of the frame, as shown.

27 Continue, gluing in sections from strut to strut. Turn the shade around and glue the other end. Once the glue is dry, remove the pins and trim the fabric down to the ring. A raggedy edge would be visible once the light is on, so leave a neat clean edge which sits just at the 'horizon' of the ring.

LAMPSHADE STITCH

Lampshade stitch is designed to hold the fabric flat and not slip as you release tension in between stitches. The finished look is a neat zigzag row. Sew along the outer edge of the rings rather than the top. You must sew through the binding tape to secure the fabric.

1 Bring your needle out at A, in at B and out at C.

2 Bring your needle back to B and out at C. This extra stitch locks the thread in place and prevents slipping.

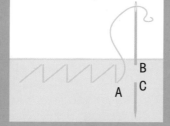

CUTTING OUT THE LINING FABRIC

If you are new to lampshade making, I advise you to use a stretchy and forgiving lining fabric such as cotton jersey. Fine cotton jersey diffuses light beautifully and, as it is very stretchy, does not have to be cut on the bias, so is more economical.

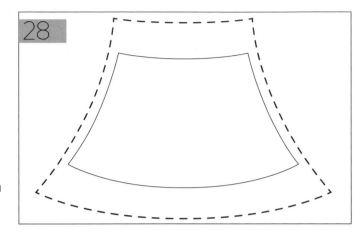

▶ **28** The same template is used for cutting out both the top fabric and the lining. Lay your jersey fabric wrong side up on your cutting surface. Position your template square to the grain of the fabric, allowing about 1.5cm (⅝in) seam allowance at the side seams and 6–10cm (2½–4in) extra at the top and bottom of each half.

▶ **29** Mark the side seam using a removable fabric marker or a tacking/basting stitch. Indicate the top edge of the template with a mark or tailor's tack. Do not mark the top or bottom edges. As you are only cutting two halves, you only need to mark up one side in this way.

▶ **30** Cut out leaving a 1.5cm (⅝in) allowance at the sides and 6–10cm (2½–4in) at the top and bottom edges.

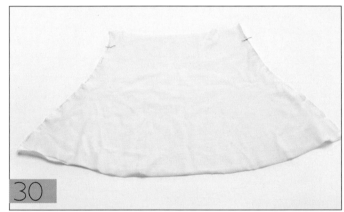

SEWING THE JERSEY LINING

▶ **31** Place the two halves together and pin along the marked side seams. Position pins at 90°. Thread your machine with matching thread and a stretch/ballpoint needle. Set the machine to a fairly small stitch length. Sew along the line, flowing in from the edge of the fabric, not the start of the marked line (see step 17, page 27). As this jersey will be stretched far more than a non-knitted fabric, it is most important to work stretch into this sewn line as you work. There are two ways to do this. Pull the fabric taut as you stitch along it, but be careful not to let it drag against the movement of the walking foot. This takes practice. Alternatively, set your machine to work a very shallow zigzag stitch rather than straight stitch. When pulled, this will become a straight line.

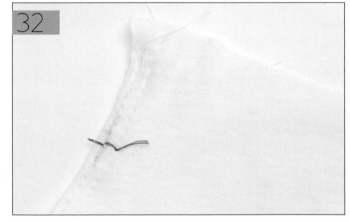

▶ **32** Then sew a second line, just 2mm (¹⁄₁₆in) to the inside of the first. This double line helps give extra strength to the seam and helps prevent fraying when pulled. Once stitched, remove the fabric marker pen, leaving the small mark or tailor's tack at the top of the template to help guide you when you fit the lining to the shade.

Idea

From jersey, you can progress onto other lovely lining fabrics such as cotton lawn, linen voile and habotai silk – but note that all these will have to be cut on the bias just like the top fabric.

FITTING THE LINING

▶ **33** Turn your shade upside down. Holding the inside-out lining by the bottom edge, drop it within the shade frame, lining up the side seams with those on the top fabric.

▶ **34** When the markers at the top edge of the lining are in line with the top ring, fold the bottom edge of the lining outwards over the bottom ring and pin in place at each vertical strut.

▶ **35** Turn the shade over and pin the top edge of the lining to the top ring, lining up the markers with the top edge and spreading the tension evenly around the circumference of the ring. Note that the gimbals will be in the way but just ignore them at this point. Turn the shade upside down again and pull tension into the lining. At this point the pins should be spaced about 2cm (¹³⁄₁₆ in) apart.

▶ **36** Turn the shade the right way up. Now that there is some tension in the semi-fitted lining, you can cut the fabric to fit around the gimbal fittings. Mark the fabric using a pencil or soluble pen dot exactly at the place where it should meet the gimbal. You may need to remove a couple of pins at either side to give you access.

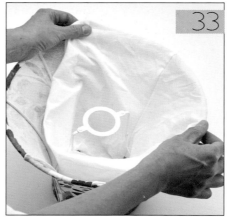

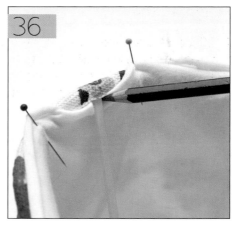

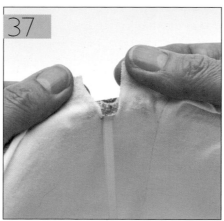

▶ **37** Cut down from the top edge of the fabric to this dot. Bring the cut fabric up to either side of the gimbal and pin neatly.

▶ **38** Repeat for all of the gimbals, and pin securely around the top ring. You can leave the gimbals like this, or trim them with ribbon or bias-cut fabric strips (see page 34).

TRIMMING THE GIMBALS

The stage at which you trim the gimbals depends on whether the lining or top fabric is fitted first. If the lining is fitted before the top fabric, as shown right, it is best to trim the gimbals before the top fabric is in place. In this way, the top fabric will neatly cover the raw ends of the gimbal trimming. If the lining is fitted after the top fabric (as in the example we are working through), fit the gimbal trimming after the lining is in place. The final braid around the top of the shade will cover the raw ends.

A short length of bias binding (see page 69) or ribbon is used to trim the area where the gimbal fits the top ring, hiding any raw edges neatly. Simply cut a length of ribbon, tape or bias binding to about 12cm (4¾in). Slot under the gimbal wire and bring back to the top ring, folding neatly. The two sides should lie edge to edge to prevent bulk. Stitch or glue to the front face and trim the excess from the ends.

▶ **39** With the top edge fully pinned, you can turn the shade over once more and pull extra tension into the lining fabric to create a taut balloon lining. Again, start with the seams and pull until the fabric starts to resist your tension. Naturally jersey can stretch enormously, but do not overstretch it. You are looking for a nice firm touch that pings back rather than buckles when poked. The side seams should line up with the vertical struts behind them.

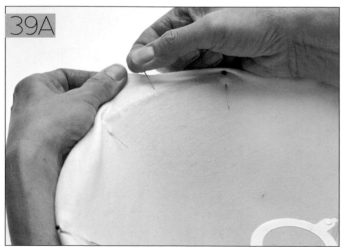
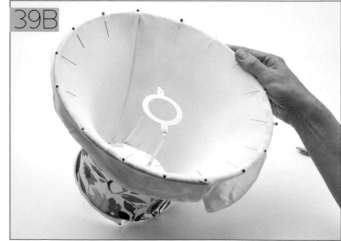

40 In this example, the lining is glued to the frame rather than stitched, in the same way as the top fabric. Working in sections from strut to strut, apply the glue to the outer edge of the wire rings. Make sure the glue line is on the wire, not creeping up on to the unsupported fabric above.

41 Pin the lining fabric into place.

42 Once dry, remove the pins and trim the lining down to the wire frame so that the raw edge will be hidden by the braid trimming.

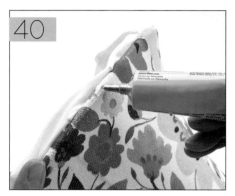

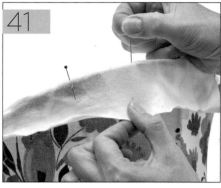

TRIMMING WITH BRAID

To finish, the raw edges will need to be covered with a decorative braid – the fun bit! A scalloped shade is best trimmed with a gimp braid, which is designed to hug curves on the flat. However, the rings of this bowed empire shade are straight, giving a far wider choice – in this case I chose tassel braid trim and velvet dressmaking ribbon.

43 Start at a side seam. Fold the end of the braid over using a tiny dab of glue to hold the fold. Apply a short line, about 2cm ($^{13}/_{16}$in), of glue along the top edge of the ring, under where the braid will sit. Position and pin the folded end into place.

44 Now glue around the ring. If the distance isn't too far, you can go almost all the way around, stopping just before the final seam. If it is big and hard to manage, do a section at a time. Once glued, carefully press the braid to the top edge, running your finger over the surface to help bind the glue. Take great care to line the braid up carefully – a wonky line will be obvious. Snip the braid just 2cm ($^{13}/_{16}$in) longer than required and fold, pressing the fold together with a tiny dab of glue. Apply glue to the last length of the ring, position and pin.

45 To finish, I covered my braid with a velvet ribbon trim, applied in the same way.

MULTI-PANELLED RAG-BAG SHADE

This lampshade is perfect for a fabric hoarder: treasured scraps of multi-coloured fabrics can be shown off, while a boldly striped pleated frill ties the anarchic palette together. The scallops kick the pleated frill out at each turn, giving a lovely silhouette.

CHOOSING THE RIGHT FABRIC

The success of this shade is in the boldly contrasting colour palette and the large scale of the patterns. Technically, it works best if the chosen fabrics are a similar weight, so that they will have similar 'give' when stretched and will allow a similar quality of light through. I used furnishing-weight fabrics. Your striped trim fabric will need to hold a crease well when pressed.

You will need

» A scalloped empire shade frame
» Cotton India tape
» Old sheeting
» Selection of top fabrics of similar weights
» A striped light- to medium-weight cotton or linen fabric
» Cotton jersey lining fabric
» Quick-dry, clear all-purpose glue
» Bead-headed pins
» Sewing kit

BINDING THE FRAME

▶ 1 Bind the shade frame as explained on pages 22–23. You will need to bind the top and bottom rings permanently. You will also need to temporarily bind two opposite verticals to create a template for the lining, and two adjacent verticals to create a template for the top fabric panels. You will remove the binding from the vertical struts once the templates are made.

MAKING A TEMPLATE

▶ **2** Make a template for the lining using the two opposite bound vertical struts. See the instructions on pages 23–25. Cut out this template and put to one side.

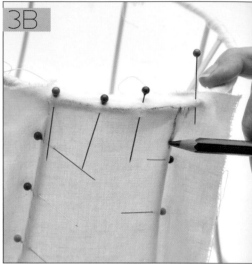

▶ **3** Make a template for the top fabric panels. This time you are pinning your sheeting fabric to the two adjacent verticals. As the main curve of this shape is from top to bottom only, pin on the sheeting with the grain of the fabric on the straight, not on the bias. This will give a more accurate template, as the fabric is less likely to stretch out of shape.

CUTTING THE OUTER FABRIC

▶ **4** The eight outer fabric panels should each be cut out on the bias and marked up ready to pin together: allow an extra 1.5cm (⅝in) of fabric at each side seam, and 5cm (2in) at the top and bottom for handling. Mark the side seam using a removable fabric marker pen or tacking/basting stitches. Indicate the top edge of the template with a mark or tailor's tack. Before pinning, spend a little time deciding in which order to arrange the fabrics. Contrasting colours will be more dramatic placed side by side.

PINNING AND SEWING THE TOP FABRIC

▶ **5** Place two panels right sides together and pin along the marked side seam. Ensure that the markers at the top of each seam tally. Position pins at 90°. Sew along the line, starting from the edge of the fabric, not the start of the marked line. Ease stretch into this sewn line as you work (see page 27, step 17). Then sew a second line, just 2mm (1/16in) to the outside of the first. This double line helps give extra strength to the seam. Trim the excess seam allowance to 3mm (⅛in) from the outer stitch line. Make your cutting line neat and sharp, as raggedy edges will be visible when the shade is lit.

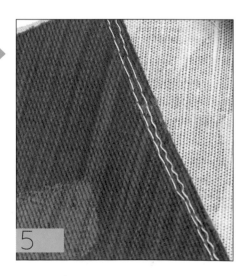

▶ **6** You will end up with a top cover that looks like a multi-panelled skirt.

FITTING THE LINING

Following the instructions on pages 32–35, pin, sew and fit the lining to the shade frame. Remember to remove the binding from the vertical struts before you start.

FITTING THE TOP COVER

Work on a clean work surface and have plenty of bead-headed pins to hand.

▶ **7** Pin and stretch your top fabric to the shade frame as described on pages 27–30. On this multi-panelled shade, it helps to pin at the top and bottom of each seam before starting to stretch the fabric. This will help to prevent it twisting.

▶ **8** Once you are happy with the fit and have checked that each seam lines up with the vertical strut behind it, you are ready to glue or stitch the top cover in place (see page 31). Either way, ensure that the glued or stitched surface sits towards the back of the ring, so that it will not be visible. Trim off the excess fabric neatly.

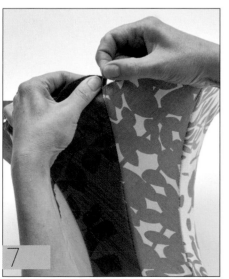

7

8A

8B

MAKING A STRIPED, PLEATED FRILL

The crowning glory of this shade is its oversized pleated frill, which kicks out at the corner of each scallop and looks like a spinning top.

▶ **9** To calculate the width of the strip of fabric, decide on the required finished depth of pleat, in my case I wanted 4cm (1½in). Double this measurement and then add 3cm (1¼in): in my case this results in 11cm (4¼in).

▶ **10** The length of fabric for the pleated frill depends on the depth and placement of the pleats, which is likely to vary to accommodate the striped pattern of your fabric. Experiment with a few variations before deciding. This pleat required triple the circumference of each ring.

▶ **11** Cut out your fabric strips and join them together, pattern-matching the stripes. Fold in half lengthways, wrong sides facing, and press with a hot iron to hold this crease.

▶ **12** Pleat the folded fabric strip, following the stripes.

▶ **13** Pin each fold, as shown.

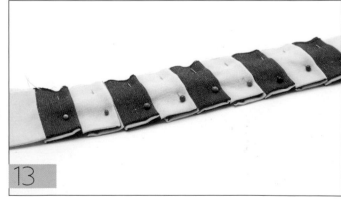

42

14

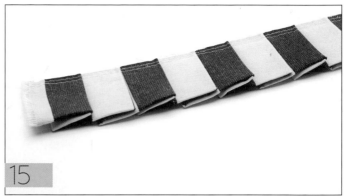

15

▶ **14** Once the full length of the strip is pinned, hand tack/baste the folds into place with large stitches. It is worth tacking/basting along the top and bottom edges to hold the pleats firmly. If you don't do this, the fabric is likely to move as you stitch and your frill will not look as neat. Remove the pins.

▶ **15** Position pins along the length of the strip, to indicate your sewing line. Here, the visible pleat will be 4cm (1½in), so the pinning line is 4.25cm (1¾in) from the folded bottom edge. Machine sew along this line using long stitches. Take care that the folds stay in line. Then sew a second row of stitches just 5mm (¼in) above the first. Trim back to 5mm (¼in) away from the stitched line.

ATTACHING THE FRILL

▶ **16** Glue the frill to the inner edge of the shade, positioning it so that the stitch line is hidden just inside the 'horizon'. Work one scallop at a time and use plenty of pins to secure the frill as it dries.

▶ **17** The two ends should join at the corner of a scallop to ensure the join is not noticeable. To join the two ends, allow a little overlap before trimming off the excess. Tuck in the raw edges of both ends; a small hand stitch at the bottom edge should hold the fold. Then glue the ends in place, arranging the pleats so they look like a continuous line of striped frill.

▶ **18** As an optional finish, consider covering the raw edge of the frill with a simple gimp braid. Cutting the edge of the frill with pinking shears prevents fraying.

16

17A

17B

SILVER SHELLS SHADE

This silk lampshade shows off a classic handmade shell ruffle trim in all its glory. This impressive trim is made by simply hand stitching a zigzag line along the length of a strip of silk fabric and then gathering it up into large shell-like ruffles. Be brave with proportions – in this case, size does matter.

You will need

» A tall bowed empire shade frame
» Cotton India tape
» Old sheeting
» Top fabric: silk dupion is ideal
» Lining fabric: either silk or cotton jersey
» Quick-dry, clear all-purpose glue
» Bead-headed pins
» Sewing kit

» Note: this trimming is especially greedy in fabric: about 33cm (13in) of fabric was used to make the fitted cover for one shade, whereas double that amount – 66cm (26in) – was used to make a deep ruffle trim.

COVERING THE SHADE FRAME

▶ **1** Following the method used on pages 23–25, create a template for your shade frame. This tall empire shade required just two panels of fabric, therefore I bound the top and bottom rings (see pages 22–23), and temporarily bound two opposite vertical struts in order to make a template that covered half the frame.

▶ **2** Use the template to cut out, sew and fit your silk outer cover to the frame, following the full instructions on pages 26–31. (For useful tips on working successfully with silk, see the tip on page 46).

▶ **3** Use the same template to make a lining for your shade. I used lightweight antique white cotton jersey fabric. A habotai silk would also work well. Fit the lining following the method described on pages 32–35. Glue the taut lining into place then trim to a neat edge. Trim the gimbals using strips of silk dupion (see page 34). The shade is now covered and lined, ready to be embellished with your handmade shell ruffle trimming.

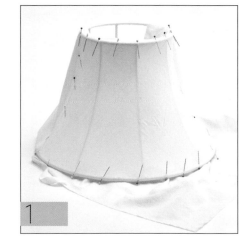

1

3A

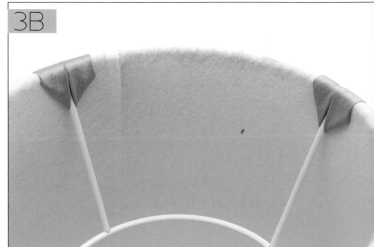

3B

Silk dupion looks wonderful and has plenty of give on the bias so it should be fairly straightforward to use. The challenge is that the sheeny surface shows up every flaw, wrinkle and pucker, so perfection is required. Pay extra attention to achieving a very tight fit, and do not let pins scar obvious holes in the silk. Once fitted, never be tempted to pick up or handle a silk shade by anything other than the metal frame, as any dimples or ripples you make will not ease away.

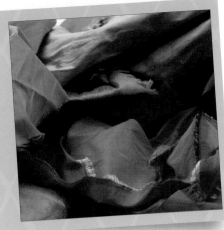

MAKING SHELL RUFFLE TRIMMING

The shell ruffle trimming is made from a tube of fabric, pressed so that the seam is at the centre back. Here is how to calculate the size of the strips.

▶ **4** For these 40cm (16in) tall lampshades, the width of the finished strips is 7cm (2¾in). To calculate how wide to cut your fabric to make the strips, double the required finished width and then add 2cm (¹³⁄₁₆in). In this case the cut fabric strips were 16cm (6½in) wide.

▶ **5** To calculate the length, measure the circumference of each ring and triple it. Here, the top ring measured 40cm (16in), so I required 120cm (48in); the bottom ring measured 60cm (23½in), so I required 180cm (70½in).

JOINING STRIPS

For all but the smallest shades, you are likely to need to join at least two strips together. To make the join as discreet as possible, it is better that the join is diagonal rather than straight across the strip:

▶ **6** Place the two ends right sides together at a 90° angle. Sew diagonally across the join, from edge to edge. Trim off the excess and press the seam open.

▶ **7** Once opened the join will give a straight strip with a diagonally sewn line across, which will all but disappear from view when the strip is gathered up.

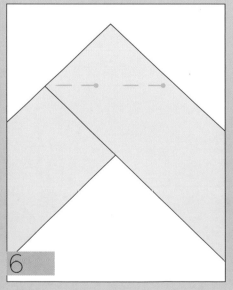

6

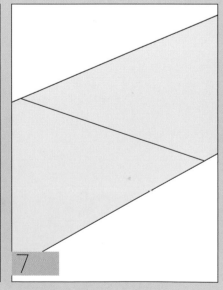

7

8 Once you have your strips of joined fabric, make them into tubes. Fold the strips in half lengthways, right sides together, and pin, using the pins to mark out your sewing line, 1cm (⅜in) from the long raw edge. Machine sew along the line, removing the pins as you go.

9 Trim to neaten. Use the tip of an iron set to 'silk' heat, to press open the seam. Use a large safety pin (I use a knitter's stitch holder) to turn the tube the right way out: pin it to one end of the tube…

10 … then post it back through the tube to turn it right side out.

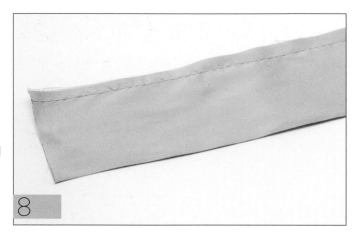
8

48

9

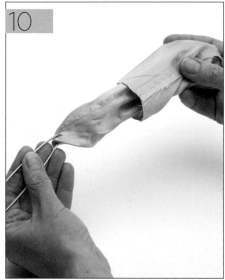
10

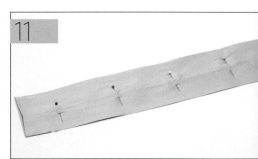
11

11 Press the tube flat, ensuring that the stitch line is at the centre back. Turn the raw ends in and press. Mark along the length of the tube with evenly spaced pins; they should be the same distance apart as the width of the strip. In this case, 7cm (2¾in).

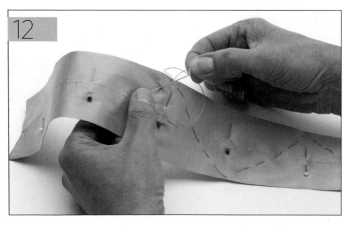
12

13

12 Using the pins as a guide, work a zigzag line of running stitch along the length of the strip. Use the pins to guide you, aiming for the pin heads and tips at each point of the zigzag. It is vital that your length of thread is longer than the strip, otherwise you won't get to the end before needing to gather it up. Choose a quality strong thread to help prevent breaking or tangling. Start with a large firm knot at the back.

13 Gather up the fabric, pushing the ruffles along the strip as you go. Be gentle to avoid breaking the thread. Once the strip is the right length, ease the ruffles along to arrange them evenly. Check the length of the ruffle again against the circumference of the lampshade, before making a couple of stitches to secure the thread.

ATTACHING THE TRIMMING

14 Check that the ends of the ruffle trim are neatly tucked in.

15 Pin one end of the trim to the ring at a side seam.

16 Carefully run a bead of glue around the rim of the ring, starting 2.5cm (1in) after the side seam. Take care that the line of glue isn't too thick or dribbly. I usually glue halfway round.

17 Now wrap the length of ruffle trim onto the ring, positioning it carefully and holding it with enough tension so that it sticks to the glued ring.

18 Once you reach the end of your glue, pin to hold.

19 Finally, glue the rest of the way around, stopping 2.5cm (1in) before the last side seam. Pin to hold. Now you have the two ends meeting at the side seam. Glue the last section and arrange the ends so that they butt up together nicely, then pin. Repeat for the other ring.

14

15

16

17A

17B

EMBROIDERED VINTAGE TABLE-LINEN SHADE

Evocative of an era when tea time involved a pretty dress and time for small talk, hand-embroidered table linen is rarely used today. Rather than leave it folded away, what could be a better way of showing it off than on a lampshade? Your template will position the four embroidered corner motifs evenly around the shade, creating a beautiful connected design. Any old tea stains – often found in the centre of the cloth – will be snipped away. A pretty floral lining bursts into life when the light is on, giving a vibrant new personality to this very pretty shade.

CHOOSING THE RIGHT FABRIC

To replicate this shade, you will need a tablecloth with four matching hand-embroidered corners. Each corner will cover two panels of your chosen shade frame (assuming it has the standard number of eight panels). Ideally the table linen will be in good condition with no holes or visible tea stains. To line the shade, choose a fine lawn or patchworking-weight cotton fabric that picks out the embroidery colours. In this project you will see several different fabric examples being worked, to show how different the same design can look when made using different tablecloths.

You will need

» A scalloped or bowed empire shade frame
» Cotton India tape
» Old sheeting
» A hand-embroidered tablecloth
» A floral cotton fabric – lawn or patchworking weight
» Quick-dry, clear all-purpose glue
» Bead-headed pins
» Sewing kit

BINDING THE FRAME

▶ **1** Bind the shade frame as on pages 22–23; you will need to bind the top and bottom rings permanently. You will also need to temporarily bind two opposite verticals to create a template for the lining, and two struts that are two panels apart to create a template for the top fabric panels. These vertical struts will be unbound once the templates are made.

MAKING THE TEMPLATES

▶ **2** Make a template for the lining using the two opposite vertical struts. Follow the instructions on pages 23–25. Cut out the template pieces, then put aside.

▶ **3** Now make a template for the top fabric panels. This time, pin your sheeting fabric to the verticals with two panels in between. Cut out this template and draw around it to make another version in tracing paper.

CUTTING THE EMBROIDERED LINEN TOP FABRIC

52

▶ **4** Lay the clean pressed linen tablecloth on a clean flat surface, smoothing it out so that it is square. Position the tracing-paper template over one of the embroidered corners, positioning it to find the portion of embroidery that you want to show off. If the design is symmetrical, a centre line drawn on the template will help ensure the design is evenly balanced. Pin into place.

▶ **5** Use a soft pencil to mark the key sections of the embroidery design on the tracing-paper template. Pay particular attention to any elements of the design that meet the sides. Finally, hand sew a tacking/basting line along the edge of the template to mark the sewing line. Sew a tailor's tack at the top corners.

▶ **6** Reposition the template onto the next corner, marrying up the drawn-on elements on the template with the embroidered design beneath. Again, ensure that any elements meeting the sides line up in the same place. Once again, hand-tack, chalk or pin around the outline of the template on the cloth to indicate the sewing line, sewing tailor's tacks to the top corners. Continue until you have marked up all four corners. Cut out the pieces, leaving a 1.5cm (⅝in) seam allowance along the side seams and around 5cm (2in) finger-pulling room at the top and bottom.

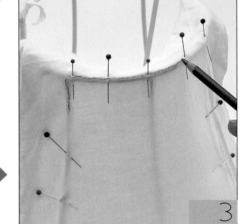

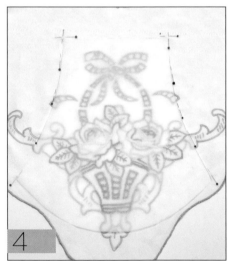

PINNING AND SEWING THE TOP FABRIC

▶ **7** Pin these four sections together along the hand-tacked/basted sewing line. Ensure that the tailor's tacks at the top corners are lined up, plus any sections of embroidery that should meet along the side seams, as this will give a pleasingly continuous design.

▶ **8** Now machine sew along the hand-tacked/basted lines using a thread to match the linen cloth. Start from the edge of the fabric, and ease stretch into this sewn line as you work. Then sew a second line, just 2mm (¹⁄₁₆in) to the outside of the first. Finally, trim the excess seam allowance to 3mm (¹⁄₈in) from the outer stitch line, making your cutting line neat and sharp.

7A

7B

MAKING AND FITTING THE LINING

▶ **9** Following the instructions on page 32, and using the template you created in step 2, create a lining from the floral lining fabric. After removing the bindings from the vertical struts, pin and fit the floral lining to the shade frame, with the right side facing inwards. Either sew or glue the lining in place (see page 31), then trim the edge of the lining close to the top and bottom rings, leaving a neat edge.

9

FITTING THE TOP COVER

Work on a clean work surface and have plenty of bead-headed pins to hand.

▶ **10** Trim your gimbals, following the instructions on page 34.

▶ **11** Pin and stretch your top fabric to the shade frame as described on pages 27–30. For this four-panelled cover, it helps to pin at the top and bottom of each seam, easing tension into these seams to hold them straight before starting to pin and tighten the rest of the fabric. This will help prevent twisting. Vintage well-washed linen usually has plenty of give and fits well without wrinkling.

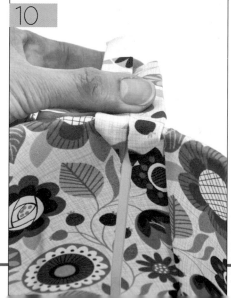
10

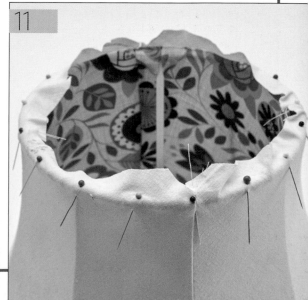
11

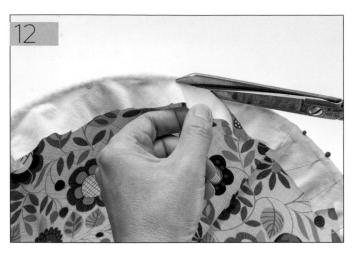

12 Once you are happy with the fit and have checked that each seam lines up with the vertical strut behind, glue or stitch the top cover in place (see page 31). Ensure that the glued or stitched surface sits towards the inside of the ring, so that it will not be visible. Trim off the excess neatly to leave a clean horizon.

MAKING A FLORAL PLEATED FRILL

▶ **13** To calculate the width of the strip of fabric needed, decide on the required finished depth of pleat, in this case 2cm ($^{13}/_{16}$in). Double this measurement and then add 3cm (1¼in): 7cm (2¾in).

▶ **14** The length of fabric for the pleated frill depends on how overlapped the pleats are. Experiment with a few variations before deciding. In this case, the pleats are 1cm (⅜in) deep with a 1cm (⅜in) gap between them, so the length of the fabric strip needs to bc double the circumference of the ring.

▶ **15** Cut out your fabric strip. You may need to join several strips if your lampshade is quite big. Press flat and turn out any seams. Fold in half lengthways, wrong sides facing, and press to hold this crease.

▶ **16** Position pins along the length, 2cm ($^{13}/_{16}$in) apart.

▶ **17** Fold and repin the fabric, using the pins as a guide, to create the 1cm (⅜in) pleats. Press the folded strip again, aiming to keep the pleats neat and even. At this stage you could hand tack/baste the pleats into place.

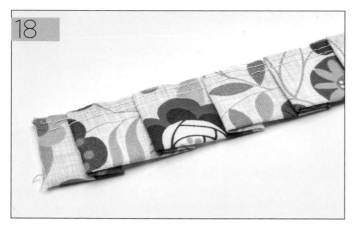

▶ **18** Machine sew along the top edge of the pleated strip, sewing two lines, the first 2cm (¹³⁄₁₆in) from the folded edge, the second nearer to the cut edge. Trim to give a neat edge close to the top line of stitching.

TIP: If you sew so that the strip feeds through with the folded edges facing backwards at the top and forwards underneath, the pleats are less likely to be crumpled by the machine's foot.

ATTACHING THE FRILL

▶ **19** You now need to glue the frill to the inner edge of the shade, positioning it so that the stitch line is hidden below the horizon. Work just one or two panels at a time and use plenty of pins as you go. Start by pinning the frill in place, about 1cm (³⁄₈in) from the end.

▶ **20** Fold back the frill, then apply a thin line of glue to the edge of the frame.

▶ **21** Work around the shade, section by section, securing and pinning the frill in place. To join the ends, allow a little overlap before trimming off the excess. Tuck in the raw edges of both ends; a small hand stitch at the bottom edge should hold the fold. Then glue the ends in place, arranging the pleats so they look like a continuous line (see below).

▶ **22** Cover the raw edge of the frill with a simple gimp braid if you wish.

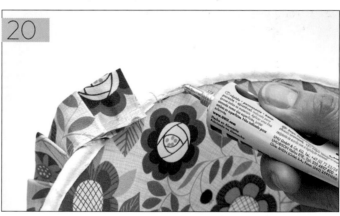

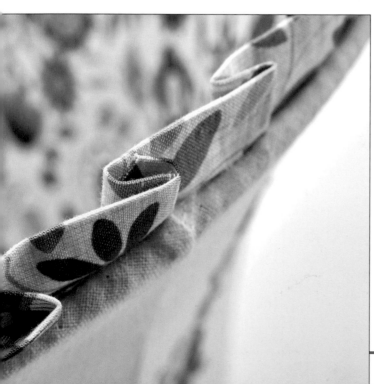

WOOL ORIGAMI SHADE

Thick woolcloth is an unusual choice for lampshade making but, just like paper, it doesn't fray when cut and holds its weight, which makes it perfect for origami-inspired sculpting.

CHOOSING THE RIGHT FABRIC

The success of this shade depends on choosing a wool fabric that will have much the same qualities as felt. It shouldn't fray when cut, should be created from a woven rather than jersey fabric, and will be stiff enough to hold its shape. Upholstery-weight woolcloths are often the best. The pleasure of this shade is all in the folded details, so plain rather than patterned cloth works well.

BINDING THE FRAME

▶ **1** Bind the shade frame as explained on pages 22–23. You will need to bind the top and bottom rings permanently. You will also need to temporarily bind two opposite verticals to create a template for the lining, and two side-by-side verticals to create a template for the top fabric panels. These vertical struts will be unbound once the templates are made.

MAKING A TEMPLATE

▶ **2** Make a template for the lining using the two opposite vertical struts. See the instructions on pages 23–25. Cut out this template and put to one side.

▶ **3** Now make a template for the top fabric panels. This time you are pinning your sheeting fabric to a single panel. Pin on the sheeting with the grain of the fabric on the straight, not on the bias – you will find this will give a more accurate template as the fabric is less likely to stretch out of shape.

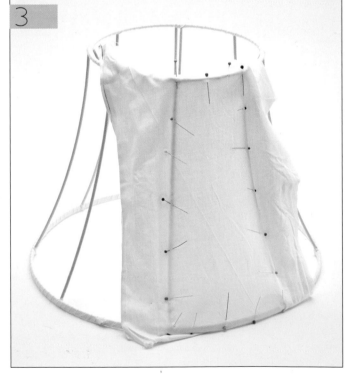

56

CUTTING OUT THE TOP FABRIC

▶ **4** Use the template to mark up and cut out the eight top fabric panels. These panels should each be cut out on the straight of the grain of the fabric. Leave a 1.5cm (⅝in) seam allowance along the side seams and approximately 4cm (1½in) top and bottom to allow finger-pulling room for fitting and pinning.

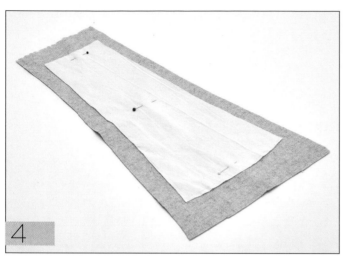

PINNING AND SEWING THE TOP FABRIC

▶ **5** Mark up the sewing lines with either tailor's chalk or a hand-sewn tacking/basting line. Sew a tailor's tack at the top of the template onto each side seam (see page 27). This will enable you to line up each piece correctly when pinning together. Pin all eight pieces together, wrong sides facing. Pin along the marked sewing line, ensuring the tailor's tacks meet up along the side seams. If you have left a 1.5cm (⅝in) seam allowance, you can use this as a guide to pin each piece together accurately.

▶ **6** Machine sew along the tacked/basted (or chalked) sewing line, removing pins as you sew. Sew from the top to bottom edges, the full length of each seam. Ease stretch into this sewn line as you work (see page 27, step 17). As this sewn line will be visible, choose a quality matching thread and be as straight and tidy as possible. A fairly long stitch length looks good.

▶ **7** Now trim the seams, making your cutting line neat and sharp. The cut seam allowances should be an even width along their length, 1–1.5cm (½–⅝in), depending on the size of the shade. Mark this first with pen to ensure you cut an even seam allowance.

FITTING THE TOP COVER

Work on a clean work surface and have plenty of bead-headed pins to hand.

▶ **8** Pin and stretch your top fabric to the shade frame as described on pages 27–30. It helps to pin at the top and bottom of each seam, lining it up with the vertical struts, before starting to stretch the fabric. This will help to prevent it twisting. Line up the seams with the vertical struts. For a good, firm pinned fit, position a pin on either side of each seam, top and bottom. This encourages the seam to sit neatly while you work.

▶ **9** Once you are happy with the fit and have checked that each seam lines up with the vertical strut behind it, you are ready to glue or stitch the top cover in place (see page 31). Either way, ensure that the glued or stitched surface sits towards the back of the ring, so that it will not be visible. Each seam should be positioned splayed outwards, as shown. Once glued or stitched, trim off the excess neatly.

FITTING THE LINING

▶ **10** Following the instructions on pages 32–35, pin, sew and fit the lining to the shade frame. Either glue it or stitch it in place (see page 31) then trim off the excess neatly.

MAKING AN ORIGAMI-STYLE TRIM

The crowning glory of this shade is its three-dimensional structured frill, which gives the otherwise plain frame an eye-catchingly unusual silhouette. Happily, it's far easier to make than it looks. First, decide on the proportions of the frill. For my 28cm (11in) high by 40cm (15¾in) wide shade, I decided to make a frill 7cm (2¾in) deep. I wanted seams of 1cm (⅜in) spaced every 5cm (2in) along the length, and a central sewn line sewn 3cm (1¼in) from the top edge.

▶ **11** The length of the fabric strip for your trim will need to be approximately one and a half times the ring circumference. The height should be the required height (e.g. 7cm/2¾in) plus a further 2cm (¹³⁄₁₆in) to allow you to trim back to give a neat finished edge. So, if my finished trim needs to be 7cm (2¾in) high by 100cm (39in) long, the fabric strip required to make it will be 9cm (3½in) high by approximately 1.5m (59in) long. Cut a strip of fabric for your trim.

▶ **12** Position pins along the length, indicating the position of each cut seam, including in this calculation the depth of each seam. You will add on an additional 2cm (¹³⁄₁₆in) for each seam, so in this case your measurements will be 7cm (2¹³⁄₁₆in) apart.

▶ **13** At each pin, fold the fabric and re-pin, with a 1cm (⅜in) seam allowance.

▶ **14** Sew along the length of each folded seam in matching thread, 1cm (⅜in) from the fold.

▶ **15** Snip neatly along the centre of each fold. Do not iron.

▶ **16** Pin the seams open, following the required line of sewing to spread the seams apart (I chose to position mine 3cm/1¼in from the top).

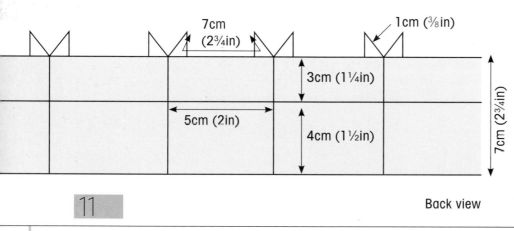

7cm (2¾in)

1cm (⅜in)

3cm (1¼in)

5cm (2in)

4cm (1½in)

7cm (2¾in)

11

Back view

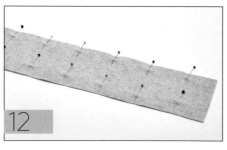

12

13A

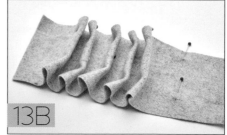

13B

14

15

16

17 Sew along this pinned line neatly in a straight line. Carefully trim back the top and bottom edges to ensure they are straight and even.

ATTACHING THE ORIGAMI TRIM

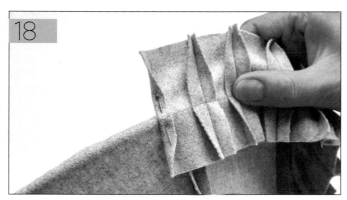

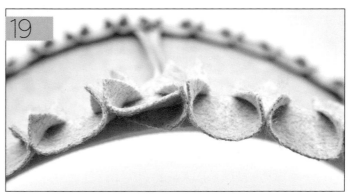

18 The trim is easily attached to the covered shade with glue. Run a neat fine line of glue along the edge of the ring and pin the trim to it, easing it on with a slight amount of tension along the length and pinning regularly.

19 A little easing should enable you to ensure that two cut seams meet at the join, allowing you to join them invisibly by tucking one end into the other, as shown.

MACHINE-EMBROIDERED SHADE

Drawing 'freehand' with the machine foot – just as you would with a pencil – is great fun and not nearly so tricky as it appears. These wonderfully spindly seed heads are simple stitched lines 'drawn' over appliquéd fabric shapes. When lit, the design bursts into life.

WHAT IS FREE-MACHINE EMBROIDERY?

Free-machine embroidery is drawing using your sewing machine. By lowering the teeth, or feed dogs, which push the fabric along under the foot, you are free to twist, turn and move the fabric freely, letting the needle 'sketch' lines. Free-machine embroidery can be used to draw linear patterns or to 'colour in' areas. In this design, it is used to draw over appliquéd pieces of patterned fabric. Most sewing machines have a switch to lower the feed dogs – often positioned behind or underneath the machine.

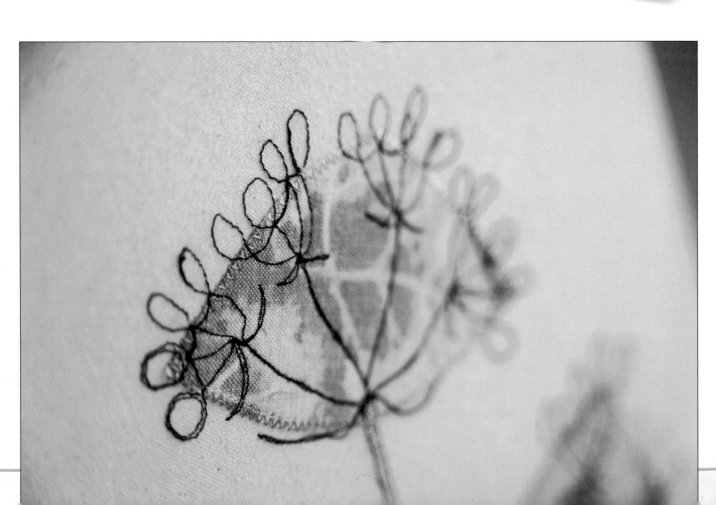

CHOOSING THE RIGHT FABRIC AND THREAD

To emphasize the machine-embroidered design, the chosen background fabric is a simple plain natural calico. Each seed head comprises a patch of patterned fabric appliquéd to the background fabric to give colour, and drawn over with machine embroidery to give detail. Lightweight finely woven fabrics glow when the light is on, whereas thicker fabrics may be dull or grainy. Select pattern and colour that will not distract from the embroidery by being too bold or busy. Before you start, play with different variations until you find something that works for you.

MAKING THE MACHINE-EMBROIDERED PANELS

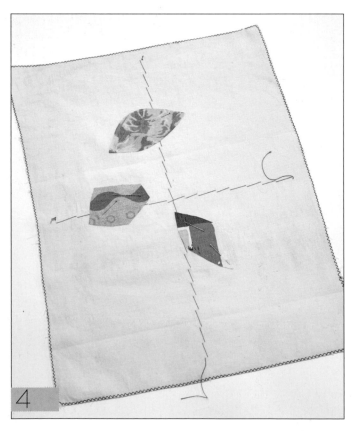

PREPARING THE FABRIC PANELS

▶ **1** Cut out the fabric panel to be machine embroidered at least 10cm (4in) larger all the way around than the required finished size. The fabric panel will be square to the frame, with the warp and weft running vertically and horizontally, not diagonally.

▶ **2** Tack/baste a centre line both horizontally and vertically on the fabric panel. This will help you position the appliqué pieces correctly.

PREPARING THE APPLIQUÉ PIECES

▶ **3** Trace the shapes of the seedheads from the patterns provided (see page 66) and use these to cut out patterned fabric pieces. Label them 1, 2 and 3 and mark the top of each piece to ensure you place them the right way up.

▶ **4** Iron fusible webbing to the reverse of each piece. Position on the fabric panel and iron to attach in place.

MACHINE EMBROIDERY

GETTING STARTED

▶ **5** Sew around the appliquéd fabric pieces with a medium-width zigzag stitch. Here, the thread matches the base fabric. If you are appliquéing bright coloured fabrics, sew the edges in matching bright thread.

▶ **6** Prepare your machine by dropping the feed dogs (teeth) and fitting a darning foot. Always work with the foot down while stitching. The fabric should be held tight and straight while you work, to help prevent puckering – the best way to do this is to use an embroidery ring frame. Bind the inner ring with cotton India tape as this helps grip the fabric. Put the fabric panel into the frame. See below for machine-embroidery tips, and page 67 for the technique.

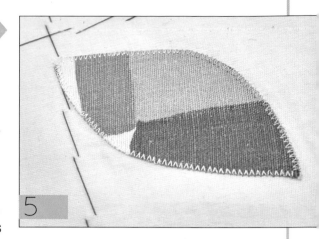

5

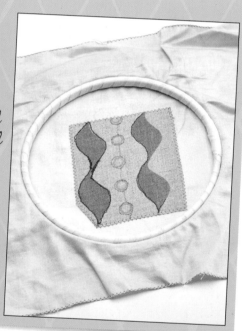

FREE-MACHINE EMBROIDERY TIPS:

* Have a scrap piece of the same fabric to hand to test out tensions and stitch variations before each stage. If you can have one ready prepared in a ring frame, even better.

* Because you are working over two layers of fabric, you may need a stronger machine needle than usual.

* The sample piece (right) shows practice of machine embroidering by following the outline of a pattern on fabric. It's a good exercise to do to get into the swing of it, and check your tensions and stitch length, before tackling the real thing.

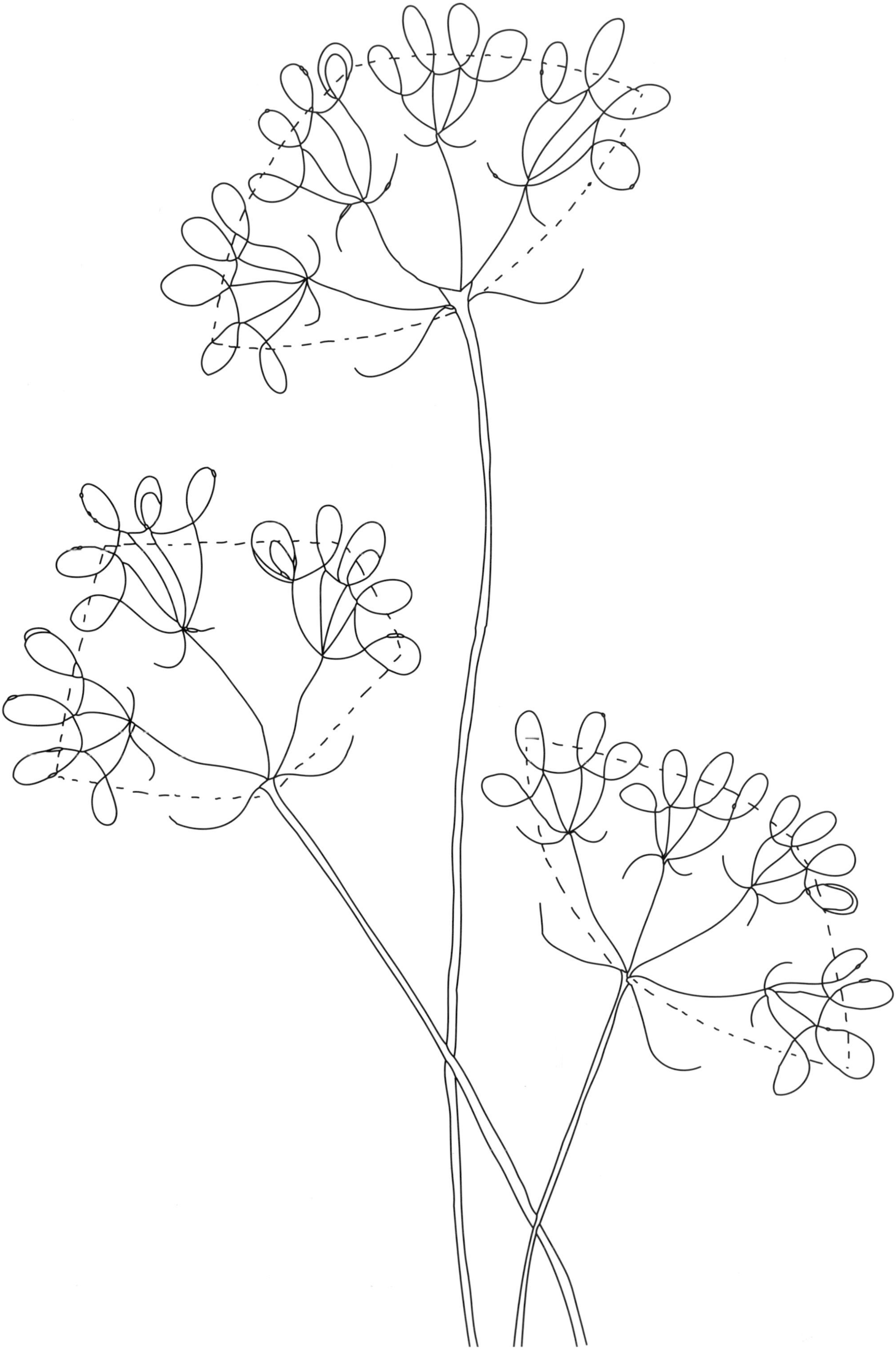

MACHINE EMBROIDERING THE SEED HEADS

▶ **7** Machine embroidering is just like drawing with a pencil, except rather than move a pencil over paper, you are moving fabric under a needle. It is far better to relax and enjoy it, so do some practice lines, twists and turns on your spare piece before you start the actual embroidery.

Study the given tracing and illustration (see left and right) to see the journey the drawn line takes, from bottom left in a continuous loopy line around the seed head to the bottom right. Each seed head is quite quick to do once you get going. You may find it helps to tailor's chalk the three key elements of each seed head onto the fabric to help position your embroidery.

To start, slide the ring frame under the machine and drop the presser-foot lever. Work steadily around the design, keeping the needle moving at a regular speed and moving the ring frame steadily to create the drawn line. Once all the seed heads are stitched, use a hand sewing needle to bring the loose ends from the front to the back of the work and trim off.

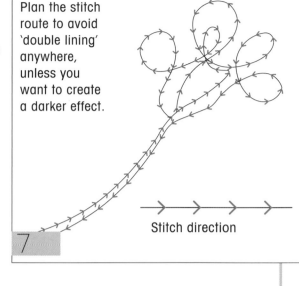

Plan the stitch route to avoid 'double lining' anywhere, unless you want to create a darker effect.

Stitch direction

7

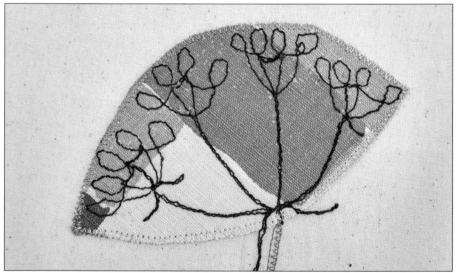

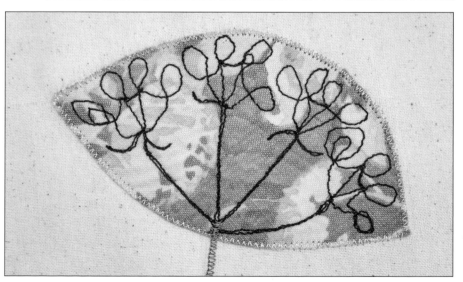

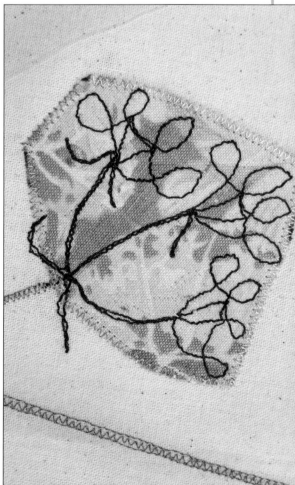

MACHINE EMBROIDERING THE STEMS

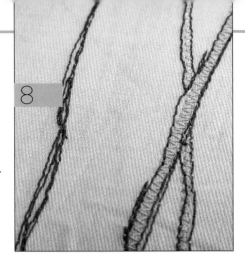

▶ **8** Put the standard sewing foot back on and raise the feed dogs of your sewing machine. Using a medium-width zigzag stitch and a coloured thread to suit, zigzag stitch the stems. Again, you may find it easier to lightly chalk the stems onto the fabric before you start. Now work the outline of the stems in a straight machine stitch. In this case I have used black thread to match the seed heads.

▶ **9** To finish, use a hand sewing needle to bring any loose threads to the back of the work, and trim off. Iron carefully on the back.

COVERING THE LAMPSHADE

Once the embroidery is finished you can use it to cover your shade frame, in this case a simple straight-sided rectangular shade.

▶ **10** Start by binding the top and bottom rings (see pages 22–23), then temporarily bind the two verticals of one side panel. As the panels are essentially flat and straight-sided, it makes sense to pin a piece of paper to the shade to make the pattern, rather than fabric, as this will ensure you have an exact replica of the actual shape.

▶ **11** Use the template to cut out the fabric panels. The front and back panels should be cut out on the straight of the grain, whereas the side panels should be cut on the bias (see diagrams, right). This will help you ease and stretch the cover into position.

▶ **12** The lining is a four-way stretch cotton jersey and is cut out on the straight grain. Make up the lining using the method described on page 32.

▶ **13** Cover the frames with the embroidered top cover first (see pages 27–31). Next, trim the gimbals using fabric or bias binding (see page 34).

▶ **14** Attach the lining (see pages 33–35).

▶ **15** Finish the shades using a handmade bias binding made from the base fabric. Instructions for making bias binding are given opposite. To attach the binding, first choose where the join should be. In this case, the join is at the back, near to one corner. Start by pinning one end to the shade. This end should not be folded in, as this will create unnecessary bulk. Run a very fine line of glue around the ring, onto the fabric where the bias-binding trim will sit. Carefully ease the bias binding trim onto the glued surface, pulling it a little taut and taking great care to ensure it sits in a straight line. Add pins occasionally as you work, although the tautness of the trimming should ensure it does not slip. It is best to work with the trim at eye-level. Stop just 2.5–5cm (1–2in) before you reach the other end. Fold the end over at an angle, sloping down from the top edge (or up from the bottom edge). Hold this fold in place with a small smear of glue and then stick the end down, holding in place with a pin until set.

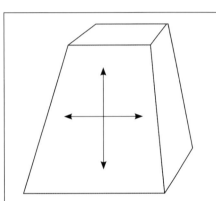

Front and back panels: direction of warp and weft.

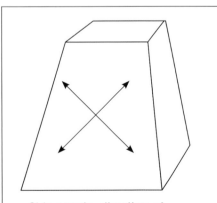

Side panels: direction of warp and weft.

MAKING YOUR OWN BIAS BINDING

▶ **1** Cut a strip of fabric diagonally across the grain of the fabric. This 45° angle allows the fabric strip to stretch. The strip should be three times the width of the required finished bias binding. So, if you need a 1.5cm (⅝in) wide bias-binding trimming, cut a 4.5cm (1⅞in) strip. Note that bias-binding trimming is pulled a little taut when applied to the shade, so it will narrow slightly. If you need to join strips together to make the required length, join the strips at an angle (as shown) as this will be less visible.

▶ **2** Use an iron to press the strip, folding approximately the first third inwards.

▶ **3** Repeat with the other edge to create a 1.5cm (⅝in) strip. Marking up with chalk is time-consuming and often unnecessary. The first fold can be done by eye while still maintaining good accuracy. The second fold can be marked with pins or checked along the length with a ruler to ensure you maintain a constant 1.5cm (⅝in) finished width.

HAND-EMBROIDERED GIFT SHADE

What could be more gorgeous than a handmade lampshade as a first birthday gift? Hand embroider a child's drawing on pretty linen, or embroider their name. This beautiful and easy-to-make idea will make a timeless heirloom gift. This design is stitched in sweet-shop shades on fine pink linen. When lit, the drawing bursts into life.

CHOOSING THE RIGHT FABRIC AND THREADS

To show off the hand embroidery best, the background fabric should be finely woven and plain, such as linen shirting fabric.

Happily, embroidery silks (actually cottons) are available in hundreds of shades, so you are bound to find just the right colour. This drawing design was worked in two strands of embroidery thread. Before you start, play with different variations until you find something that works for you.

THE RIGHT DESIGN

A simple name in confident swirly script, a copy of a child's drawing, simple flowers and shapes copied from a favourite story book… all are easy to achieve and effective for being simple.

▶ **1** To create the template for your fabric, and the space in which you can plan your design, follow the technique explained on pages 23–25. Start by binding the top and bottom rings, and then temporarily bind two side-by-side verticals to create a template for each side panel.

▶ **2** If you want to use the same designs as me, see page 73. If you want to create your own, practise on several pieces of paper until you get your design right. Make sure the design is evenly spread and that any words can be read clearly. Try out colours as well, to work out what you want. Ensure you leave at least 1cm (⅜in) free around the design to allow for the seam allowance.

PREPARING THE FABRIC PANEL FOR EMBROIDERY

▶ **3** Cut out the fabric panel to be embroidered at least 6cm (2½in) larger all round than the required finished size. The fabric panel will be square to the frame, with the warp and weft running vertically and horizontally, not diagonally. It may help to chalk, or tack/baste, the outline of the shade frame on the fabric before positioning the design.

▶ **4** Trace the design on to the fabric. You can do this using carbon transfer paper to trace a removable line onto the fabric. Alternatively, tape the design onto a window or lightbox. Position the fabric over it and trace through using a water-soluble pen.

EMBROIDERING THE DESIGN

▶ **5** Put the fabric into an embroidery ring frame, centring the traced design. The ring frame will hold the fabric taut, to help keep your stitching at an even tension. Binding the inner ring with cotton India tape will help grip the fabric.

▶ **6** Backstitch following your traced design (see below). Aim to keep your stitches the same size throughout. Do not be tempted to bring thread across the back of the fabric between motifs, but tie off properly and restart each time.

BACKSTITCH

Backstitch is a great embroidery stitch for beginners and a useful stitch for many small hand-sewn projects. The stitch is so-called because you start a stitch length into your line and then stitch back to the beginning. Tie a small knot in the end of the thread to keep it from pulling out.

▶ **1** First decide on the length of your stitches; bring your needle up that distance from the starting point along your stitch line at A.

▶ **2** Complete your first stitch by bringing your needle and thread back through your fabric at the starting point of the line (B).

▶ **3** Move on to the second stitch. Bring the needle up through the fabric an equal distance in front of your first stitch (C). Aim to make each stitch the same size. If stitching around curves, smaller stitches will help smooth the line; for straight lines, longer stitches will work.

▶ **4** Complete the second stitch by bringing the needle back through at the original starting point. This keeps your stitches in a continuous line and prevents gaps.

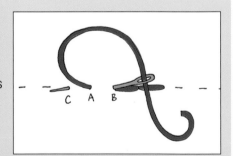

COVERING THE LAMPSHADE

Once the embroidered panel is finished you can use it to cover your shade frame.

▶ **7** Use the template to cut out the fabric panels. The embroidered front panel is cut out on the straight of the grain. The curve of the shade means that the side seams of this front panel will be partially on the bias of the fabric, helping you ease and stretch the cover into position. Sew the four panels together, following the technique used on pages 26–27. The usual seam allowance for the side seams is 1.5cm (⅝in). Once sewn with two rows of machine stitching, the excess seam allowance can be trimmed back to 2mm (¹⁄₁₆in) behind the sewing line. It is vital that this excess seam fabric is trimmed away, otherwise it will show as a dark shadow when the light is on. Fit the top cover following the instructions on pages 27–30. Ensure that the side seams line up with the vertical struts beneath before gluing or stitching the cover into place.

▶ **8** The lining is a four-way stretch cotton jersey, cut on the straight of the grain. Make up the lining using the method described on page 32, and attach it using the detailed instructions on pages 33–35. Once glued or stitched into place, trim back the excess fabric, ready to be finished with a decorative trimming.

TRIMMING THE GIMBALS

▶ **9** Before finishing the edges of the frame with a trimming, wrap a short length of bias binding around the top of each gimbal (see page 34). This gives a neat finish and hides any raw edges. It can be glued or stitched onto the front edge of the covered ring.

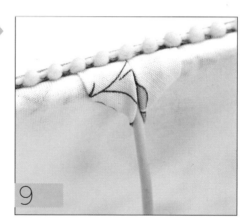

TRIMMING WITH POMPOMS AND BRAID

▶ **10** A tiny mini pompom braid is used to trim the edges of the shade frame. The pompoms are positioned to sit along the top edge, like castellations. Like most trimmings, it did not have particularly decorative tape, so I covered it with a bias binding made from a coordinating fabric (see page 69). The overlap of the bias binding trimming is out of view at the back of the shade; I positioned it in a corner to make it as unobtrusive as possible, tucking the ends in at an angle for a neat finish.

WOOLLY TWEED SHADE

Woolcloth, tartan and tweed – warm, thick, fuzzy… and rarely associated with lampshades. This shade is a lot of fun – with its mismatched multicoloured tweedy scraps – and makes the most of an interesting banded shade frame.

You will need

» A banded shade frame
» Cotton India tape
» Old sheeting
» Selection of wool and tweed fabrics of similar weights
» Cotton jersey lining fabric
» Embroidery and sewing threads in colours to match the fabrics
» Wool yarns to make tassels
» Fine 2- or 3-ply yarn for crocheted edge
» Quick-dry, clear all-purpose glue
» Bead-headed pins
» Sewing kit

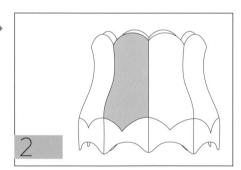

CHOOSING THE RIGHT FABRIC

Warm thick wools and tweeds have never traditionally been part of the lampshade maker's repertoire. However, despite their thickness, they diffuse light well, with the hairiness of the cloth giving an additional halo of light. The simple open weaves and natural softness of the yarn allows plenty of give on the bias – a great boon to the lampshade maker. Wool fabrics are also highly forgiving when handstitched – absorbing stitches with little or no puckering – essential when some panels are to be sewn by hand.

MAKING THE TEMPLATES

▶ **1** Bind the shade frame as explained on pages 22–23. You will need to permanently bind all the horizontals (top ring, and both bottom rings), plus the short vertical struts between the two bottom rings. You will also need to temporarily bind two adjacent verticals to create a template for the top fabric panels, and two opposite verticals for the lining template. These verticals will be unbound once the templates are made.

▶ **2** As on page 38, create a template for the individual panels, excluding the bottom band section, using the two adjacent bound verticals, the top ring and the top ring of the band. Cut out pieces of fabric roughly to size for each section of the bottom band – cut about 2cm (13⁄16 in) larger all round.

Template for an individual top panel.

▶ **3** Create a template for the lining using the two bound verticals opposite each other and the top and bottom rings. This creates a lining with just two seams.

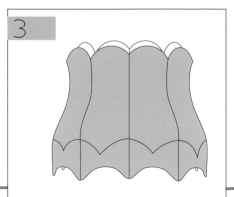

Template for a 2-seam lining covering half the shade frame.

CUTTING YOUR FABRICS

▷ **4** Now it's time to cut out the eight top fabric panels. Each panel will be cut on the bias, which means that on the finished shade the tartan fabrics will be diagonally checked. Take time to position the templates over the fabrics to choose the best variations of pattern and colour. Mark up the side seams using a removable fabric marker pen or tacking/basting stitches. Stitch a tailor's tack on each side seam to indicate the top of the panel, which will enable you to line each panel up when pinning together. When cutting out each panel, allow an extra 1.5cm (⅝in) fabric at each side seam, and 4–6cm (1½–2½in) at the top and bottom for handling. Before pinning the panels together, spend a little time deciding in which order to arrange the fabrics.

4

SEWING THE TOP FABRIC

▷ **5** Place two panels right sides together and pin along the marked side seam. Ensure that the markers at the top of each seam tally. Position pins at 90°. Sew along the line, starting from the edge of the fabric, not the start of the marked line. Ease stretch into this sewn line as you work (see step 17 on page 27). Then sew a second line, just 2mm (1/16 in) outside the first. This double line helps give extra strength to the seam. Trim the excess seam allowance to 3mm (1/8 in) from the outer stitch line. Make your cutting line neat and sharp, as raggedy edges will be visible when the shade is lit. When all eight panels are joined, you will end up with a top cover which looks like a multi-panelled skirt.

5A

5B

FITTING THE TOP COVER

Work on a clean work surface and have plenty of bead-headed pins to hand.

▶ **6** Pin and gradually stretch your top fabric to the shade frame as described on pages 27–30. It helps to pin at the top and bottom of each seam before starting to stretch the fabric. This will help prevent it from twisting. To navigate the vertical struts around the bottom band, snip along the sewn seam up to the ring, as shown. The double-stitched seam should prevent the seam from unravelling further than intended. This will allow you to fit your cover around the vertical struts, as shown.

▶ **7** Once you are happy with the fit and have checked that each seam lines up with the vertical strut behind it, you are ready to glue or stitch the top cover in place. Either way, ensure that the glued or stitched surface sits towards the back of the ring, so that it will not be visible (see page 31).

SEWING THE BAND

The individual panels for the band are fitted and stitched in place by hand. It is best to attach four alternate panels first, then the remaining four.

▶ **8** Pin the fabric taut over alternate panels as shown.

▶ **9** Glue or stitch the bottom and sides to the frame (see page 31). Tuck the remaining (top) edge in and pin, keeping the fabric taut.

▶ **10** Use a curved needle and matching thread to slip stitch the fabric to the adjoining side panel.

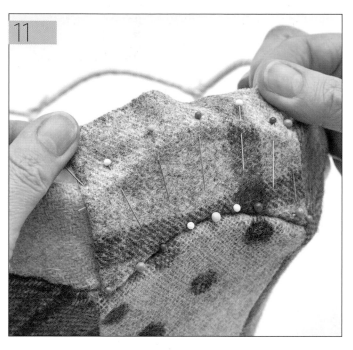

11 Once the first four panels are in place, attach the next four. This time, three of the edges will be tucked in and stitched, and just the bottom edge will be turned under the frame and stitched or glued. As you work, keep the inside neat, trimming back the excess fabric and gluing or stitching to the inside of the frame to prevent ugly silhouettes when the light is on.

MAKING A CROCHET PICOT EDGE

A fine crocheted edge is in keeping with the woolly theme and gives a neat finish to the shade. This is done by blanket stitching around the top and bottom edges of the shade into the wool fabric and then crocheting into the blanket-stitch loops.

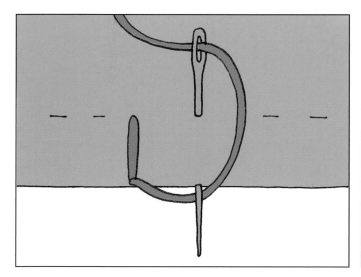

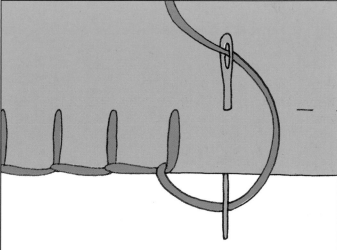

12 Thread your needle with embroidery cotton and knot the tail end. Bring up your needle from the back, about 5mm–1cm (¼–⅜in) from where you want your stitches to be. To anchor the stitch, push the needle up from the back again in the same place, creating a loop around the edge. Push the needle through the stitch you just made at the edge of the shade, where you want your loops to sit. This anchors the thread, but is not a true blanket stitch.

13 Push the needle down from the top. Bring your needle up from the back and through the loop of thread. This creates a straight line. Draw the thread tight. Continue, making evenly spaced blanket stitches right around the edge of the shade. Before adding the crochet edging, see Lining the shade on page 82.

PICOT CROCHET

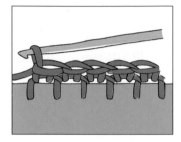

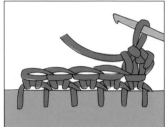

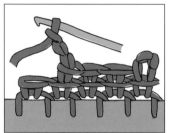

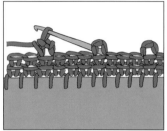

▶ **14** Work along the blanket stitch, making one UK dc (US sc) stitch into each blanket stitch loop. If the loops are widely spaced, you may need to make two stitches per loop. Fasten off the yarn when you reach the end.

▶ **15** At the start of your second row, chain three and then make one UK dc (US sc) stitch in the base of the chain. This is your first picot.

▶ **16** To continue, work three UK dc (US sc) stitches along the row, then chain three again and make one UK dc (US sc) back into the base of the stitch.

▶ **17** Continue along the edge of the frame.

LINING THE SHADE

For best results, fit the lining after fitting the top cover and blanket stitching the edges, but before crocheting or adding the tassels; for clarity in the photographs I have shown the stitching without the blanket-stitch edge in place. Cut out and then fit and pin the lining to the inside of the shade as described on pages 32–35. The pins should be pointing inwards, with the bead heads sitting around the inside of the top and bottom rings.

▶ **18** Trim the excess fabric down to just 5mm (¼in) and turn this edge under. Work in small sections, just removing one pin at a time to avoid loosening the tension of the lining. Once all the raw edges are neatly turned under, carefully sew this edge to the frame using a neat ladder stitch and a small curved mattress needle.

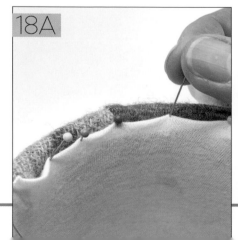
18A

18B

18C

MAKING TASSELS

Each of the eight points around the bottom edge of the shade are embellished with a fabulously fat wool yarn tassel. As with the fabric, an assortment of coloured yarns is used. The finished tassels are simply stitched to the corner points of the shade frame to secure in place.

▶ **19** Cut a piece of card about 2cm (¹³⁄₁₆in) deeper than the required finished length of the tassel. Start wrapping the yarn neatly around the cardboard – cutting a small slit in the card enables you to secure the end.

▶ **20** Wrap enough yarn to make a tassel of the correct chunkiness.

▶ **21** Tie a length of yarn around the threads at one end, pull tight and tie off.

▶ **22** Slide the yarn off the cardboard. Thread a large needle with a length of yarn in a different colour and push through the head of the tassel. Pull through so that the end is buried in the tassel loops. Wind the yarn length tightly around the head of the tassel until you are happy with the size of the wool collar. Re-thread the needle and push back through the collar to tie off the end.

▶ **23** Trim the length of the tassel to the required size.

Pleated projects

MAKING A PLEATED SHADE

THE CORE SKILLS

The best way to learn the art of pleated lampshades is with straight knife pleats on a shade frame with top and bottom rings of the same circumference. This means you can concentrate on creating perfectly positioned pleats without the additional complication of spacing them differently top and bottom. Here, a straight-sided oval shade is covered in silk dupion, a sumptuous sheeny fabric that holds folds well and shows off the pleated surface beautifully. Pleats take time, but shouldn't be hurried; bear in mind that they can be worked in stages.

You will need
- » A straight-sided round, oval or square shade frame
- » Cotton India tape
- » Old sheeting
- » Top fabric: silk dupion is ideal
- » Lining fabric: lightweight silk or cotton
- » Beaded trimming
- » Quick-dry, clear all-purpose glue
- » Bead-headed pins
- » Sewing kit

CHOOSING THE RIGHT FABRIC

You can check the suitability of your fabric by running your finger and thumb along a fold and seeing if it forms a sharp crease. A finely woven fabric emphasizes the pleating effect better when lit, compared to a thicker weave. Plain fabrics show off pleats better than patterns, which can look busy.

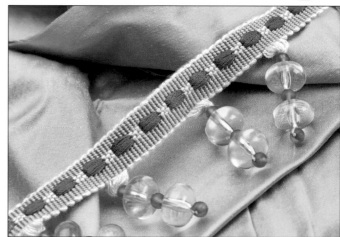

HOW MUCH FABRIC DO I NEED?

The strip of fabric you will pleat onto the frame needs to be 8cm (3¼in) more than the depth of the frame, and two to three times the circumference. Although a lot of fabric is needed, it is used on the straight of the grain, so there is little wastage. Multiple strips do not have to be pre-sewn together.

▶ **1** In order to create the lovely striped effect when the lamp is lit, the pleats on your shade need to be spaced apart, so that the three layers of the pleat create a dark stripe followed by the light single layer. If the pleats and spaces are the same width, it makes calculating the fabric amount easier, because you can just double the circumference of your lamp for the total width required. The width of the pleats plus spaces needs to fit exactly into the circumference of the lamp and evenly between two vertical struts so that you can work panel by panel. My pleats were 2cm (¹³⁄₁₆in) wide, with five pleats per panel. Use metric or imperial measurements, but don't interchange or your calculations will go wrong. The height of the fabric strips should be the height of the frame plus 8cm (3¼in) for finger pulling room. Do not trim the fabric widths yet, as you may need extra for joining.

PREPARING YOUR FABRIC

▶ **2** Trim off the selvedge from the short ends of the strips. Mark the position of the doubled pleat widths (4cm/1½in) in pencil, tailor's chalk or soluble fabric pen. The first mark should allow a foldover of about 1.5cm (⅝in).

PREPARING YOUR SHADE FRAME

▶ **3** Bind the top and bottom rings with cotton India tape (see pages 22–23). Create a lining, as described on page 32, and put to one side.

▶ **4** Mark the rings top and bottom where the pleats will be positioned with tailor's tacks, or a soluble fabric marker, each the required width (2cm/¹³⁄₁₆in) apart.

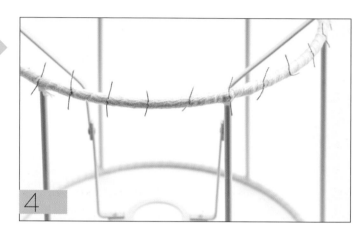

PINNING PLEATS ONTO THE FRAME

If the frame is small, you will probably work on your lap. A larger frame is easier to work standing up to a worktable, with the shade on a folded sheet to create a soft but stable surface. You will need plenty of bead-headed pins.

▶ **5** To start pleating, fold the short end over at the first pair of markers, giving a fold of around 1.5cm (⅝in). Pull the fabric taut to make a crisp pleat, which should be along the straight of the grain. Starting at a vertical strut, pin the fold to the top and bottom rings. Note the positioning of the pins (with the points facing inwards). This angle helps to hold the fabric taut and prevents you from being scratched. The fabric should be held taut between the pins.

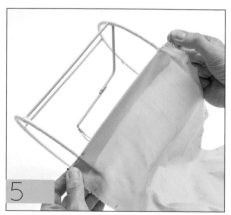

▶ **6** Continue by pinching the fabric at the next marker and pulling taut to make the next pleat. Bring this fold over to lie at the second marker on the rings, and pin. On a straight-sided frame like this, the depth of each pleat will be the same at the top and bottom. The finger handling allowance should stay the same at the top and bottom.

7 Continue around the frame, pinching and pinning the pleats in the same way.

TIP:

Regularly hold the shade over a light source to check that the pleats are even.

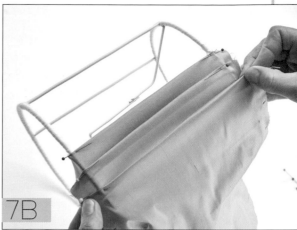

7A

7B

STITCHING YOUR FABRIC ONTO THE FRAME

By the time you have pinned pleats around one third of your shade you will be dealing with a lot of pins, and are likely to have pricked or scratched yourself. At this stage, it is a good idea to start stitching the fabric in place, so you can remove the pins. You can work around your shade like this in sections.

8 Start sewing lampshade stitch (see below) at the second pleat. It's important to leave the first pleat pinned only as it will need to be lifted to position the final pleat beneath it. Sew using an extra-strong upholstery weight thread, or double your regular sewing thread. Sew along the outer edge of the rings rather than the top. You must sew through into the binding tape to secure the fabric.

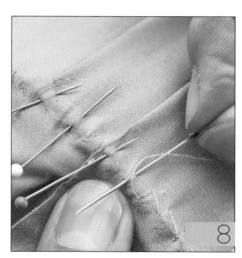

8

LAMPSHADE STITCH

Lampshade stitch is designed to hold the fabric flat and not slip as you release tension in between stitches. The finished look is a neat zigzag row.

1 Bring your needle out at A, in at B and out at C.

2 Bring your needle back to B and out at C. This extra stitch locks the stitching in place and prevents slipping.

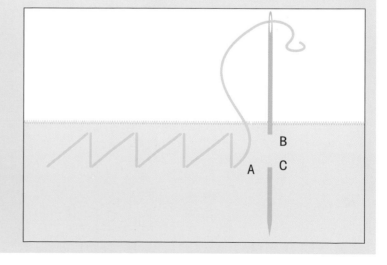

9 Remove the pins as you go to reduce the risk of your thread tangling. Do not cut off the excess fabric, as lhis is useful to hold while stitching to keep the fabric taut. As you sew the pleats in place, this is a good time to remove each tailor's tack marker, using tweezers or small snipping scissors.

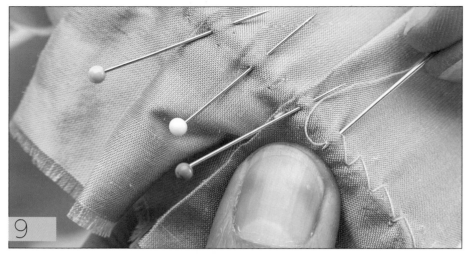

10 For larger shade frames, you are likely to need more than one strip of fabric. To start a new strip, cut out and mark up the fabric as you did previously. Trim off the selvedge and fold over the first pleat, as before. Trim the end of the previous strip so that the cut edge sits where the inner fold of a pleat would lie.

11 Take your new strip and pin the folded end over the end of the previous strip, positioned at the next marker on the frame. The new fabric strip should now look like a seamless join. At this stage it is a good idea to hold the shade up to the light to check that the folded in fabric looks like all the previous pleats, as it will show up when the bulb is lit.

12 To finish your pleating, the end of the fabric strip should sit behind the first fold. Un-pin the first fold and pin the end of the fabric strip to the frame. Trim if necessary so that the overlap is the same depth as the pleats. Re-pin the first fold over the fabric onto the frame and stitch through all layers. Trim the edges so that the fabric just wraps neatly over the rings.

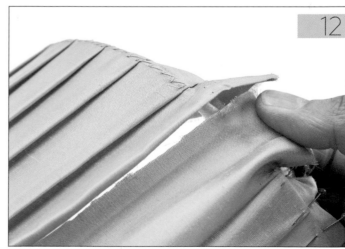

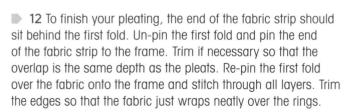

FITTING THE LINING

▶ **13** Fit and pin the lining into position, following the method described on pages 33–35. Use lampshade stitch to stitch the lining to the frame, working through as many layers as possible (see page 89). Make sure that your stitches sit on the front face of the rings, not the top edge, where they may be visible. Trim the lining just below the stitching, as shown.

13

TRIMMING YOUR PLEATED SHADE

The shade now needs trimming at the top and bottom rings to hide the raw edge of the lining. This shade is trimmed with self-made bias binding (see page 69) at the top and bottom, with an additional beaded fringe trim around the bottom edge.

14 To attach the beaded trim, pin one end of the ribbon to the bottom ring, positioning it so that the bottom edge of the ribbon sits neatly at the horizon of the bottom ring. Run a narrow band of glue around the bottom ring over the fabric. The line of glue should be unbroken but not so bulky that it dribbles. You may find it easier to glue just a third or quarter of the way around each time. Now wrap the beaded ribbon around the bottom ring, pulling it fairly taut and taking care that it is level. The glue should hold the ribbon in place, but use a few pins if necessary to prevent drooping. Once you have gone all the way around, stop 2.5–5cm (1–2in) before the start of the ribbon. Trim the ribbon to length and then glue the final section in place. Pin to secure and leave to set.

15 Make up enough bias binding to trim the top and bottom rings (see page 69). To attach the binding, first pin one end to the ring, positioning it to sit at the side of the shade. Smear the tiniest amount of glue to the ring, allowing it to go tacky before you wrap the binding over it. When wrapping the binding, ensure that it sits evenly around the ring and is pulled fairly taut as this will help it to sit neatly and hug the ring. Fold the end of the bias binding diagonally, keeping the fold held with glue. Smear a tiny amount of glue to the back of the folded bias binding and pin to the shade ring to hold.

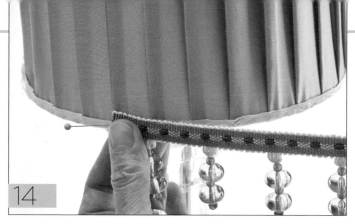

14

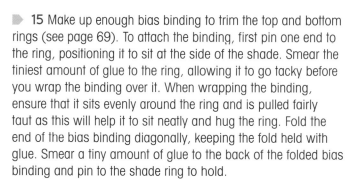

15

93

TIP:
To save pricking your fingers, use fabric plasters (band-aids) or strapping tape wrapped around your most-used fingertips.

SILK BOX-PLEATED SHADE

Box pleats are a smart variation on knife pleats and suit a shade where the bottom ring is wider than the top. Accurate spacing emphasizes the orderly arrangement and, when lit, the layers create a striking sun-ray effect. This shade is worked in purple silk dupion lined in scarlet red dupion, which glows gloriously. It is trimmed with an informal silk chiffon ruffle.

CHOOSING THE RIGHT FABRIC

Silk or cotton lawn holds a crease well, making it ideal for pleated shades. On this shade, the folds have been left loosely creased for an informal look. A finely woven fabric emphasizes the pleating when lit. Plain fabrics will show off the pleats while striped and checked fabrics will create interesting patterns; a large informal pattern may create dramatic results, but a small fussy pattern will lose the pleated effect.

HOW MUCH FABRIC DO I NEED?

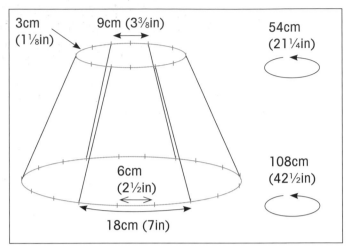

As with the previous shade, you will be pleating the fabric onto the frame. The strip needs to be a little more than the depth of the frame, and at least three times the length of the top circumference. Triple the circumference of the top ring, and double that of the bottom ring to allow for some sparseness of fabric between the box pleats to let light shine through just one layer. Although a lot of fabric is needed, it is used on the straight of the grain, so there is little wastage.

▶ **1** First, decide how wide you want each box pleat to be and then calculate how many pleats will fit evenly between two vertical struts around the top ring. For example, on this shade, the distance between two struts around the top ring is 9cm (3⅜in). So three 3cm (1⅛in) pleats will fit within each panel at the top ring. The distance between two vertical struts around the bottom ring is 18cm (6¾in), twice the size. In order to be able to work box pleats around the bottom, you will need to allow at least half as much again, in this case an additional 9cm (3⅜in). This 27cm (10⅛in) fabric per panel would allow 9cm (3⅜in) fabric per 3cm (1⅛in) box pleat. In total: 27cm (10⅛in) x six panels gives a total of 162cm (60¾in).

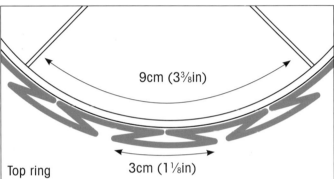

Top ring

▶ **2** To calculate the depth of the strip, measure the height of the vertical struts and add about 8cm (3¼in), allowing 4cm (1⅝in) handling room on each edge. In this case the strips were 24cm (9½in) wide.

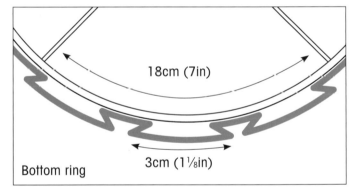

Bottom ring

PREPARING YOUR FABRIC

▶ **3** Cut a strip of fabric to the calculated depth. Leave 5cm (2in) at the start as an overlap, which will sit neatly behind the join between the first and last pleats. Mark along each edge every 9cm (3⅜in). Trim off the selvedge from the short ends of the strips. Mark along each edge every 9cm (3⅜in). Then in the middle of each 9cm (3⅜in), mark a pleat centre point, so you will see where to fold as you are working. Over time, you may find that these markers become unnecessary as you get the feel for the technique.

3

PREPARING YOUR SHADE FRAME

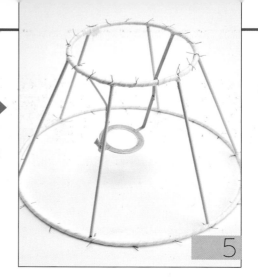

▶ **4** Bind the top and bottom rings and two opposite vertical struts with cotton India tape (see pages 22–23). Create a lining, as described on page 32, and put to one side. Remove the binding from the vertical struts.

▶ **5** Mark the top ring where the pleats will be positioned with tailor's tacks, or a soluble fabric marker. Mark the bottom ring in the same way, spacing the markers as calculated to tally with the top ring – in this case, one in line with each strut and two within each panel section.

PINNING PLEATS ONTO THE FRAME

6A

6B

You will need plenty of bead-headed pins and a clean, firm surface to work on. A folded sheet on a worktable is ideal.

▶ **6** Start pleating the fabric to the frame, working panel by panel. Note that you should allow an initial overlap long enough so that it can be tucked under the preceeding pleat when finished. Pin the fabric to the top and bottom rings aligning the 9cm (3⅜in) spacings on the fabric with the markers on the rings. It should look as shown.

6C

TIP:

Note the position of the pins. This angle helps to hold the fabric taut and prevents you from being scratched. The fabric should be held taut between the pins – aim to use plenty of pins.

7A

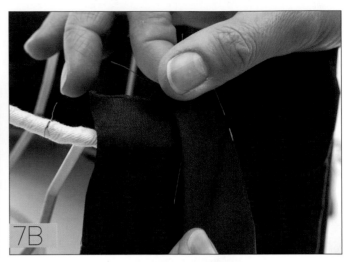

7B

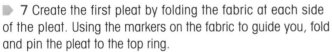

▶ **7** Create the first pleat by folding the fabric at each side of the pleat. Using the markers on the fabric to guide you, fold and pin the pleat to the top ring.

▶ **8** Pleat the fabric around the first section of the frame on the top ring.

▶ **9** Now, on the bottom ring, pull the fabric taut to help create the folds. The folds should run along the straight of the grain.

▶ **10** Once you have covered the first panel in pleats, check the arrangement, tweaking the pleats to be as evenly spaced and taut as possible.

8

9

10A

10B

STITCHING YOUR FABRIC TO THE FRAME

Once you have pinned pleats around one section of your shade, it is a good idea to start stitching the fabric in place, so that you can remove the pins before going on to pin further sections.

▶ **11** Do not cut off the excess fabric before sewing as this is useful to hold the fabric taut while stitching. Start sewing at the first pleat along the top ring. At this stage leave the preceding overlap pinned as you will need to arrange this underneath the last pleat. Sew with lampshade stitch (see page 89) using an extra-strong upholstery weight thread or use a doubled sewing thread for strength. Sew along the outer edge of the rings rather than the top. You must sew through into the binding tape to secure the fabric. Remove the pins and tailor's tacks as you go to cut down on tangling.

▶ **12** Once you have stitched around the top ring, work the bottom ring in the same way. You will probably be able to add extra tension into the pleats by pulling and re-pinning before you stitch.

▶ **13** Continue to pleat, pin and stitch your fabric, section by section, until you get back to the start. If you run out of fabric halfway around, finish by stitching the single layer to the shade frame and trimming neatly it so that it will end just 1.5cm (⅝in) behind the next pleat. Continue by starting with a full pleat, which will just overlap the trimmed end. To finish your pleating, both ends of the fabric strip should sit behind the last box pleat. Stitch the start of the strip, then pin and stitch the last box pleat over it, again ensuring that the end of the strip sits neatly behind the pleat. Finally, trim the excess fabric so that it just wraps neatly over the rings at the top and bottom.

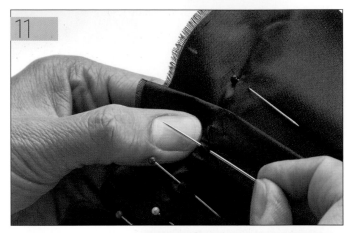

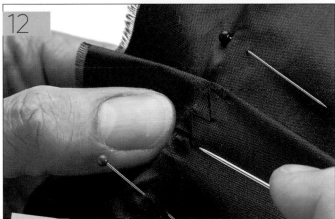

> **TIP:**
> Lampshade stitch, see page 89, is designed to hold the fabric flat and not slip as you release tension in between stitches. The finished look is a neat zigzag row.

LINING YOUR SHADE

▶ **14** Following the method described on pages 33–35, fit and pin the lining into position. Use lampshade stitch to stitch the lining to the frame, working through as many layers as possible. Make sure that your stitches sit on the front face of the rings, not the top edge where they may be visible. Trim the excess lining close to the stitching. You may prefer to use glue to attach the lining. Again, make sure that the glued surface sits in the front face of the rings, not the top edge. This photograph shows the lining after the ruffle has been attached.

CHIFFON RUFFLE TRIMMING

Silk chiffon is soft and flouncy and it doesn't crush or droop, which makes it an ideal choice for a ruffle trimming. You will need a strip of chiffon three times the circumference of each ring, and just under three times wider than the finished width of the ruffle trim. The trim on this shade is 5cm (2in) deep, so I cut strips 13cm (5in) deep.

▶ **15** Press the strip and then fold over and pin, to create a tube, as shown. Do not press the folds.

▶ **16** Using a length of extra-strong thread in a matching shade, hand sew a running stitch along the centre of the folded length of chiffon. Keep the stitch running centrally along the strip and make sure that the stitch is kept short at the front side. This will help keep it invisible, when ruffled up.

▶ **17** Draw up the fabric along the length of thread, until it is the length of the circumference of the lampshade ring.

▶ **18** Tie off the thread with a few firm stitches. Arrange the ruffles evenly along the length of the ruffle trim.

▶ **19** Attach the ruffle to the shade using pins. Take care to keep the ruffles evenly spaced. This may be fiddly, so allow time. It helps to put your shade on a lamp base at this stage, so that it is at eye level and not resting on the work surface. Once you are happy with the position of the ruffles, sew into place with a couple of small invisible stitches every 4cm (1½in). The ruffles can be nudged over to hide these stitches. If you are concerned that the trim isn't sufficiently held in place, run a very fine line of clear glue along the edge of the ring behind the trim and press the trim onto it. You will only need a tiny amount to hold it. Too much will bleed through the chiffon.

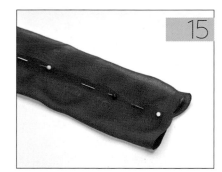

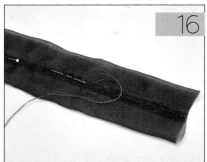

SWATHED PLEATS AND CHIFFON ROSES

Swathed pleated lampshades were the height of domestic stylishness in the mid-20th century and are enjoying a long-overdue revival. By wrapping the pleats around the shade, the curved silhouette is emphasized. Indeed, the best frames have nipped-in waistlines – all the better to show off your artfulness. Here, a classic combination of silk chiffon pleated over silk dupion is used, in striking lipstick pink.

CHOOSING THE RIGHT FABRIC

Silk chiffon has exactly the right qualities for achieving ethereally perfect pleats, with just the right amount of drape, fold and sheen, that it really isn't worth buying a faux silk, or indeed anything else. Silk chiffon is both beautifully matt and slightly iridescent. It folds, flops and drapes as required and glows gloriously when lit. Just like mixing paints, you can have a lot of fun choosing a coloured lining fabric to enhance the chiffon further. In this case, vintage peachy silk dupion warms up the sharp lipstick pink chiffon perfectly.

You will need

» A round or oval empire lampshade, ideally with emphasized waistline
» Cotton India tape
» Old sheeting
» Coloured lining fabric: silk dupion is ideal
» Top fabric: silk chiffon
» Quick-dry, clear all-purpose glue
» Bead-headed pins
» Sewing kit

HOW MUCH FABRIC DO I NEED?

The amount of chiffon needed is a little more than the depth of the shade frame, by twice the length of the widest circumference. It is used on the straight of the grain, so there is little wastage.

▶ 1 First, decide how widely spaced you want the pleats and calculate how many will fit evenly between two vertical struts. For example, on this shade, the distance between two struts is 15cm (6in) around the bottom ring. So five pleats, each 3cm (1³⁄₁₆in) wide will fit nicely. Obviously the pleats will be closer together around the top ring. Double the amount of fabric is required to make each pleat. So the length of the strip of fabric to pleat around the shade will be:

6cm (2³⁄₈in) fabric per pleat x five pleats per panel x six panels per shade = 1.8m (71¼in) per shade. You will likely need to create this length from several strips, but you do not need to pre-sew the strips together.

To measure the depth of the fabric strips, position your tape measure on the shade frame, wrapping it around as though it is following the line of a pleat. In this case, the swathe swings across two panels. Measure this height and then add 4cm (1½in) top and bottom for finger-pulling room. In this case, I needed 28cm (11in).

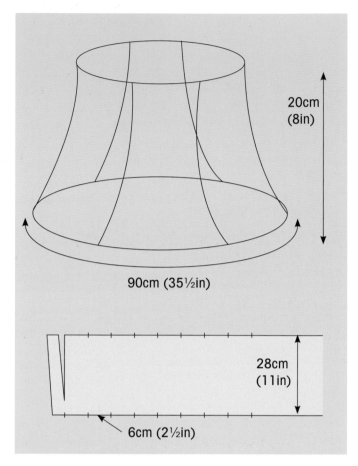

20cm (8in)

90cm (35½in)

28cm (11in)

6cm (2½in)

PREPARING YOUR FABRIC

▶ 2 Trim off the selvedge from the short ends of the strips. Mark the position of the pleats in pencil or soluble fabric pen. The first mark should allow a foldover of about 1.5cm (⁵⁄₈in).

PREPARING YOUR SHADE FRAME

▶ **3** Bind the top and bottom rings and two opposite verticals with cotton India tape (see pages 22–23). Make a two-seamed lining using your colourful lining fabric, as described on page 32, and put to one side.

▶ **4** Remove the bindings on the vertical struts. Now bind over the top and bottom rings again using strips of your lining fabric. The strips should be bias-cut and about 3cm (1¼in) wide. When binding, make sure that the trailing edge of the binding strip is turned under to hide the raw edge, as shown. The advantage of leaving the cotton India tape on is that the two layers are easier to stitch through than tightly bound silk on its own. However, if you think the effect is too bulky, you can remove the cotton India tape first.

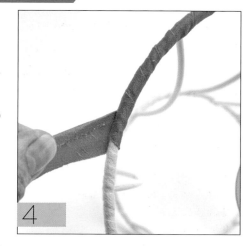

LINING THE FRAME IN SILK

Swathed pleated chiffon shades are often lined with the lining fabric stretched over, rather than under, the shade frame, like a top cover. This provides a firm surface for the relatively insubstantial chiffon to rest against, and improves the overall outline.

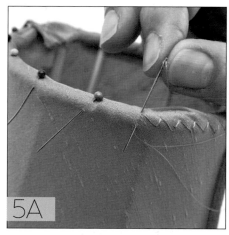

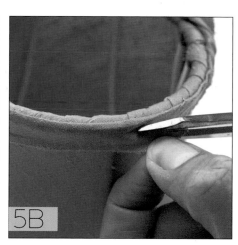

The bound rings are visible on the finished shade.

▶ **5** Following the same method as described on pages 27–31, pin and ease this lining over the shade frame. The side seams should face outwards. This lining should be sewn, not glued, into place, as it is important to turn the raw edge back over the stitches. See page 89 for lampshade stitch. Once you have turned over, trim the raw edge neatly, close to the bottom edge of the top ring.

SWATHED PLEATING WITH CHIFFON

▶ **6** Mark the position of each pleat with tailor's tacks on the top and bottom rings (see page 27). These will have to be pulled out once you've finished, so just one over-stitch should be enough.

7 Fold the end of the chiffon strip at the first marker. To start, pin the fold at the bottom ring at a vertical strut, then bring the folded pleat across two panels to the top ring, and pin at the vertical strut. Your pleat will sit diagonally across two panels. Note that sweeping across two panels is fairly usual, but for a shade with very emphasized waist, the diagonal may be across two and half or even three panels.

8 Continue pleating, taking great care to pin at the correct markers, both on the fabric strip and the shade frame. Aim to keep the overlap at the top and bottom rings the same. Pin each pleat securely as you work.

9 Once you have pleated across two panels, it's a good idea to stitch the pleats in place so as not to get overwhelmed by pins (see lampshade stitch, page 89). Do not sew the first pleat; leave it open so that the final pleat can be tucked beneath it before sewing. Sew the top ring first. When sewing the bottom ring, pull tension into each pleat, creating a crisper fold. As you sew the pleats in place, this is a good time to remove each tailor's tack marker, using tweezers or small snipping scissors.

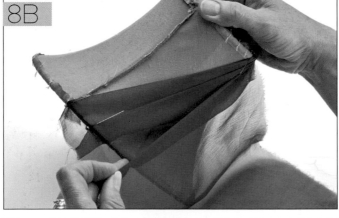

TIP:

Regularly hold the shade over a light source to check that the pleats are even.

JOINING FABRIC STRIPS

▶ **10** You are likely to need more than one strip of fabric. To start a new strip, cut out and mark up the fabric as you did previously. Trim off the selvedge and fold over the first pleat, as before. Trim the end of the previous strip so that the cut edge sits where the inner fold of the next pleat would lie. Take your new strip and pin the folded end over the end of the previous strip, positioned at the next marker on the frame. The new fabric strip should now look like a seamless join. At this stage it is a good idea to hold the shade up to the light to check that the folded in fabric looks like all the previous pleats, as it will show up when the bulb is lit.

▶ **11** Once you have pleated the whole shade frame, the end of the fabric strip should sit behind the first fold. Unpin the first fold and pin the end of the fabric strip to the frame. Trim if necessary so that the overlap is the same depth as the pleats. Re-pin the first fold over the fabric onto the frame and stitch through all layers.

▶ **12** Smear some glue along the edge of the shade frame.

▶ **13** Fold the fabric back on itself to secure in place. When dry, trim to a neat edge.

BIAS BINDING

Make up enough bias binding to trim the top and bottom rings (see page 69). Because chiffon is very light, it's a good idea to make double the length so that you can wrap it around the ring twice, making for a more robust and neat finish.

▶ **14** To attach the binding, first pin one end to the ring, positioning it to sit at the side of the shade. Smear the tiniest amount of glue to the ring, allowing it to go tacky before you wrap the binding over it. When wrapping the binding, ensure that it sits evenly around the ring and is pulled fairly taut, as this will help it to sit neatly and hug the ring.

▶ **15** To create a neat finish, fold the end of the bias binding diagonally, keeping the fold held with glue. Smear a tiny amount of glue to the back of the folded bias binding and pin to the shade ring to hold.

MAKING A CHIFFON ROSE

The crowning glory of these shades is their rose corsages: two or perhaps three roses would be wonderful. Be bold when choosing size... apologetic little buds will not suffice. Happily, silk chiffon lends itself beautifully to rolled roses, as it drapes, rolls and holds its weight without flopping. Fiddly? Yes. Worth it? Definitely!

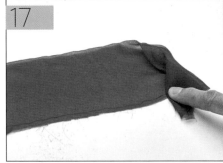

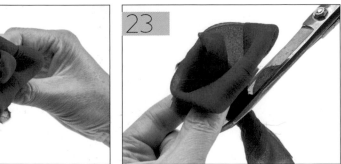

▶ **16** Start with an 18cm (7in) wide strip of chiffon. Fold it in half and tack/baste running stitches along the open edge to hold it together. Fold over the end at an angle.

▶ **17** Fold over the end again.

▶ **18** Roll this folded end inwards a couple of times.

▶ **19** Fold the strip back away from you and keep rolling. It may help to inset a pin into the 'stalk' every now and then so it doesn't unravel.

▶ **20** Just before you reach the fold, fold back away again and repeat.

▶ **21** Repeat once or twice more.

▶ **22** Once you are happy with your bloom, fold the end of the strip back. Sew a few stitches back and forth through the 'stalk' to hold everything in place.

▶ **23** Trim off the excess chiffon, leaving just enough to hold everything in place. A few invisible stitches back and forth through the rose may help hold it in place.

24 Stitch to your shade, working through just the chiffon layer using a small curved needle. Use the petals to hide the join in the bias-binding trim.

MINI GATHERED SHADES

Just like a box of sweets, a collection of tiny shades on a chandelier or wall light doesn't have to be uniform to look delicious. Here, a selection of lightweight cotton lawns from the rag bag are ruched into gathers before stitching to the frames. It's an easy, informal technique that suits small shades; these are just 11cm (4½in) high. They are trimmed in metallic gimp braids, which look like they are taken straight from the dressing-up box!

CHOOSING THE RIGHT FABRIC

Tiny lampshade proportions mean that fine lightweight fabrics are most suitable. Cotton lawn, voile and lightweight silks all work beautifully. Be brave with pattern, as the gathers break up surface pattern into a wonderful riot of colour.

You will need

» Small shade frames, straight or empire
» Cotton India tape
» Old sheeting
» Top fabric: cotton lawns are ideal
» Lining fabric: lightweight silk or cotton
» Narrow gimp braids: in this case, the sparklier the better
» Quick-dry, clear all-purpose glue
» Bead-headed pins
» Sewing kit

HOW MUCH FABRIC DO I NEED?

For each shade, you need a strip of fabric a little more than the depth of the shade frame, and three times the length of the circumference. As with most pleated shades, although a lot of fabric is needed to cover the surface area, it is used on the straight of the grain, so there is little wastage. For these shades, measuring 11cm (4½in) high by 33cm (13in) around the bottom ring, the fabric strips were 15cm (6in) deep and 1m (39in) long.

PREPARING YOUR SHADE FRAME

▶ **1** Bind the top and bottom rings with cotton India tape, and bind two opposite verticals. Create a two-seamed lining using a plain cotton fabric, as described on pages 22–25 and 32, and put to one side. Remove the cotton tape from the vertical struts.

PREPARING YOUR FABRIC

▶ **2** Sew a line of running stitches along the top and bottom edges of the strip, starting with a secure knot. The distance between the lines should be the same as the height of the vertical struts. Use strong matching thread that will not snap easily. Once sewn, leave the ends uncut and loose.

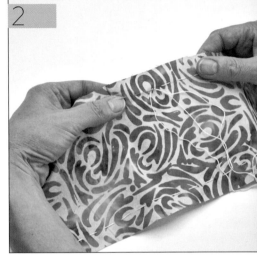

▶ **3** Place pins evenly along the two rows of stitching, one for each vertical strut. So, for my six-panel shades, there are seven pins, including one at the start and end.

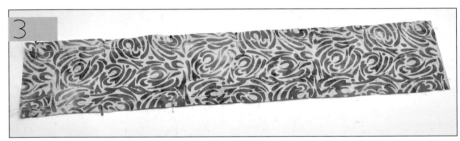

PINNING PLEATS ONTO THE FRAME

You will need plenty of bead-headed pins and a clean, firm surface to work on. A folded sheet on a worktable is ideal.

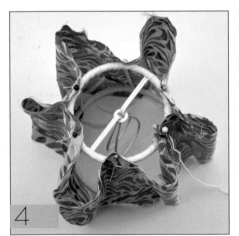

▶ **4** First, pin the fabric to the top and bottom rings aligning the pins on the fabric with the vertical struts on the rings. Each pin must bite securely through the fabric into the bound ring. Fold the two short ends in to hide the raw edges.

▶ **5** Gather up the fabric by pulling the two threads. Pull carefully and slowly. The fabric will gather up around each ring, and at first will be bunched and uneven. Tie off the thread with a few firm stitches, or lock the stitches around one of the pins, as shown.

▶ **6** Spend a little time spacing out the gathers to give an evenly ruched finish. Secure these gathers with many more pins. Aim to pull a little tautness into the fabric when pinning so that the gathers create crisp lines.

STITCHING THE GATHERS TO THE FRAME

▶ **7** Using strong matching thread, sew the fabric to the rings with lampshade stitch (page 89), working through all layers. Once you have stitched around the top ring, work the bottom ring in the same way. You will probably be able to add extra tension into the pleats by pulling and re-pinning before you stitch. Once stitched, trim the excess fabric neatly, close to the inner edge of the rings.

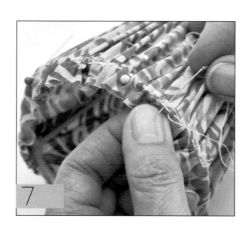

TIP:

Lampshade stitch (see page 89) is designed to hold the fabric flat and not slip as you release tension in between stitches. The finished look is a neat zigzag row.

LINING YOUR SHADE

▶ **8** Following the method described on pages 33–35, fit and pin the lining into position. Use lampshade stitch to attach it. Make sure that your stitches sit on the front face of the rings, not the top edge where they may be visible.

▶ **9** Trim the lining just below the stitches. If you decide to glue the lining in place, make sure that the glued surface sits on the front face of the rings, not the top edge.

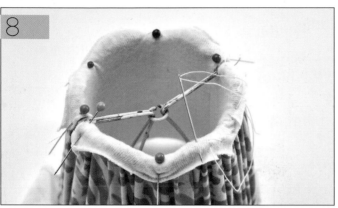

TRIMMING THE SHADE

Because these tiny shades have scalloped rings, it was important to choose a gimp braid that followed the curve of the scallops. If your shades are straight top and bottom, you will have a broader choice. In this case, I chose sparkly metallic gimp braid, but still had to ease it carefully around the curves, using lots of glue, pins and patience.

▶ **10** Start by turning under the raw end of the braid and glueing it. Starting at the valley of a scallop, glue and pin the end in place.

▶ **11** Run a narrow line of glue along the front face of the first scallop and ease the braid onto it, pinning as you go. Continue all the way around. When you get back to the start, fold in the end before gluing down.

OMBRE SWATHED GATHERS

Witty, informal and relaxed, this chic design brings a 1950s slim-waisted drum empire shade right up to date. I've swapped the traditional pleated silk chiffon for an informally dip-dyed cotton muslin, ruched on the twist, for a contemporary finish.

CHOOSING THE RIGHT FABRIC

Cotton or linen muslin fabric will dye beautifully, its lightweight gauzy weave gathers up into ruches without being bulky, and it also allows light to diffuse through… all the qualities you need. This shade is worked in humble cotton muslin, and lined in cotton jersey, which works forgivingly around the curvaceous shade frame. If you don't fancy dip-dyeing, use a plain or printed muslin, or a very fine cotton lawn instead.

You will need

» A bowed empire shade frame
» Cotton India tape
» Old sheeting
» Off-white cotton muslin
» Lining fabric: off-white cotton jersey
» Off-white cotton pompom or tassel trim
» Glass-headed pins
» Sachet of indigo cold-water dye powder
» Quick-dry, clear all-purpose glue
» Sewing kit

HOW MUCH FABRIC DO I NEED?

As with pleated shades, a lot of fabric is needed for ruching, or gathering. To measure how deep the fabric strips need to be, hold your tape measure at the top ring and take it down at an angle to the bottom ring. The angle should allow the fabric to just skim the vertical struts. The more nipped-in the waistline, the steeper the angle. For this shade, the tape measure wrapped around three panels – almost halfway around the shade – a measurement of 60cm (23½in). Add finger-pulling room of about 4cm (1½in) top and bottom to this measurement to get the depth of the fabric strip required: 68cm (26½in). The length of the strips will be the circumference of the bottom ring, multiplied by three. Unless your shade is tiny you are likely to need several strips, but these do not need to be sewn together.

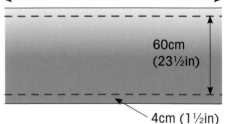

circumference of bottom ring x 3

60cm (23½in)

4cm (1½in)

PREPARING YOUR SHADE FRAME

▶ **1** Bind the top and bottom rings permanently with cotton India tape (see pages 22–23). Also bind two opposite vertical struts. Create a template then sew a lining from cotton jersey, as described on pages 23–25 and 32, and put to one side for dyeing.

DIP-DYEING THE FABRIC

GETTING ORGANIZED

Choose a dry day so you can work outside in a splash-proof place.

▶ **2** Mix up your dye sachet in a large container. Fold the top fabric strips widthways three or four times so that the folded fabric is easily clipped onto a trouser-hanger and will fit into your container without bunching up. Peg all of the strips onto the same hanger.

PLANNING THE DYE GRADATION

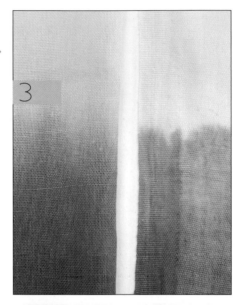

▶ **3** Although the finished effect looks relaxed and informal, it's a good idea to plan the colour change from natural off-white to deepest ink. Essentially, the fabric is divided into thirds: the top third is undyed, the centre third a mid-tone and the bottom third the strongest inky shade possible. To get this right, you might want to place pins one third and two thirds of the way up the fabric to use as visual markers. Also consider that you will get a different dye result depending on whether your fabric is wet or dry. A wet fabric will create a smoother dye graduation (see the example on the left); a dry fabric will create a more distinct line (see the example on the right).

DIP-DYEING

▶ **4** Holding the hanger, dip the fabric slowly into the dye bath until you reach the top pin, so that only the undyed section is left out of the bath. Hold there for a couple of minutes.

▶ **5** Raise the hanger until only the bottom third of the fabric is left in the dye bath. Hang your hanger on a hook – a garden chair is useful – and let the bottom third of the fabric sit in the dye-bath for about 40 minutes, or however long is recommended on the dye instructions.

RINSING... CAREFULLY!

▶ **6** Carefully remove the fabric from the dye-bath, then rinse out in cold water. To avoid any dye splashing onto the undyed fabric at the top, keep the fabric pegged to the hanger while you rinse it, avoiding touching it with inky fingers. Once the water runs clear, squeeze out most of the moisture, unpeg and hang out to dry. Iron once dry.

▶ **7** If you want to, repeat the dyeing process with the already sewn lining, dividing it into thirds as before. If you are dyeing pompom or tassel trim, immerse it into the dye bath, swishing it about to ensure that all the fibres are covered. Leave it in for the full dyeing time before removing and rinsing.

PREPARING THE FABRIC FOR RUCHING

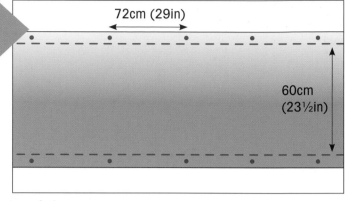

72cm (29in)

60cm (23½in)

▶ **8** Measure the distance between the vertical struts around the bottom ring and triple it. This will give you the amount of fabric to allow for each panel on the shade. On this shade the struts are 24cm (9½in) apart, so the measurement is 72cm (29in).

▶ **9** Use this measurement to pin, then stitch markers along the top and bottom edge of the muslin strips. In this case, four markers fitted along the width of each muslin strip. Trim any excess off the end, just 1cm (⅜in) past the last marker. Trim the selvedge off the other end. Repeat for each required strip.

▶ **10** Use extra-strong thread to sew a line of running stitch along the top and bottom edge of each muslin strip, starting with a secure knot. The distance between the stitched lines is the length of each swathe, calculated on page 116, in this case 60cm (23½in). Once sewn, leave the ends loose.

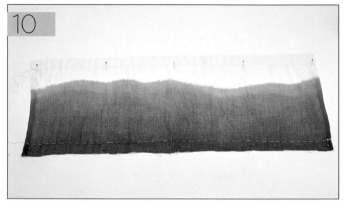

PINNING ONTO THE FRAME

You will need plenty of bead-headed pins and a clean, firm surface to work on. A folded sheet on a worktable is ideal. It is best to pin, then stitch each muslin strip into place, rather than trying to pin them all before stitching.

▶ **11** Take the first muslin strip and at the first marker, by the knot of the stitched line, pin the muslin to the top ring at a vertical strut. Then pin the next marker to the top of the next vertical strut.

▶ **12** Repeat until all the markers are pinned to the top ring, each lined up with a vertical strut. There will be a lot of bagginess between pins.

▶ **13** Now take the muslin strip at the bottom edge at the first marker. Pull the fabric around the ring to the swathed position. In this case it is three vertical struts around the ring. Pin in position at the marker. Now continue this process, pinning each marker to the next vertical strut. At this point the muslin will look baggy and disorganized, but don't worry.

14 The fabric is gathered up by pulling the two threads. Start with the top thread and pull carefully and slowly. The fabric will gather up around each section, and at first will be bunched and uneven. Once the thread is drawn tight and fits snugly around the ring, tie off with a few firm stitches. Repeat around the bottom ring.

15 Spend time spacing out the gathers for an evenly ruched finish.

16 Position pins regularly and closely around the rings. Pin the top ring first. When pinning the bottom ring, pull tautness into the fabric so that the gathers are crisp.

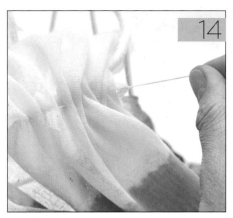

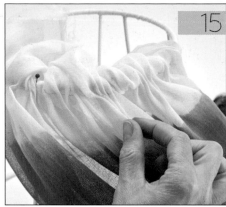

STITCHING THE MUSLIN TO THE FRAME

17 Using strong matching thread, sew the fabric to the rings with lampshade stitch (page 89), working through all layers. Once you have stitched the first muslin strip around the top ring, work the bottom ring in the same way. You will probably be able to add extra tension into the gathers by pulling and re-pinning before you stitch.

18 Once the first muslin strip is stitched in place, repeat to cover the shade frame completely, strip by strip. Where the strips join, the end of each strip should be folded in about 5mm (¼in) and the two butted up together. Once the fabric is gathered and stitched this join will disappear.

19 Once the stitching is finished, run a thin line of glue around the top of the frame and press and hold the fabric down onto this.

20 When dry, trim the excess fabric away, keeping about 5mm (¼in) away from the rings.

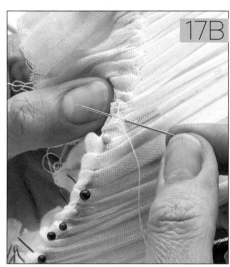

LINING THE FRAME

21 Following the method described on pages 33–35, fit and pin the lining into position.

22 Use a thin line of glue to attach the lining to the frame. Make sure your glue sits on the front face of the rings, not the top edge where it may be visible. Trim the lining just below the glued line when dry. You may prefer to stitch the lining. Again, make sure that the stitches sit on the front face of the rings. Once the lining is stitched into place and the excess fabric trimmed back, trim the gimbals using a strip of muslin (see page 34). Here, undyed muslin was used as it would not contrast with the cover fabric or lining.

THE FINAL TRIMMING

The bottom ring is trimmed with dyed tassel trim, which is then covered with bias binding made using the dyed muslin (see left); the top ring is bound in undyed muslin binding. Make up enough bias binding in both dyed and undyed shades to wrap around the rings (see page 69).

23 To attach the tassel trim, firmly pin one end to the bottom ring. Run a very thin continuous line of glue around the bottom ring, two or three panels at a time, making sure the glue sits just on the ring, not the fabric. Don't attempt it all in one go.

24 Wrap the trimming firmly onto the ring across the glue, keeping the line level. Pin at the end of the glue line. Tension should hold the trimming straight and firmly against the shade while you add a few more pins along the glued length. Continue until you are back where you started. Cut the tassel trim so that the ends butt up, glue and pin.

25 Start by pinning one end of the bias binding to the ring, either directly onto the trimming or, if on the top ring, onto the top fabric. Run a narrow line of glue around the ring, just a couple of panels along. Ensure the glue is just tacky and not dribbly before the next stage.

26 Take the bias binding and stretch it over the ring, keeping it level and taut. Pin where the glue ends. There should be no need to put extra pins in the glued-on section. Continue like this around the ring. Join with an angled end, which looks neater than a squared-off end (see below).

123

TIP:
If your fabric is fairly thin, you may find it works better to run the bias binding twice around each ring, to create a more robust finished edge.

STRIPED SWATHED CHIFFON

Boldly contrasting stripes emphasize the swathed pleated chiffon on this lampshade and bring a mid-century classic up to date. The more contrasting the fabric colours, the bolder the finished result. Time to show off!

CHOOSING THE RIGHT FABRIC

Silk chiffon has exactly the right qualities for pleating, with just the right amount of drape, fold and sheen. Its transparency allows light to shine through many layers, emphasizing all your clever work. The fun in this shade is in choosing the colours. Boldly contrasting pearl white and charcoal black make this one a classic. Or perhaps choose two colours of a different hue but similar strength – perhaps bright orange and bright pink – the effect will be just as fabulous but very different. Go on, have a play...

You will need
» An empire lampshade: the more emphasized the waistline the better
» Cotton India tape
» Old sheeting
» Lining fabric: fine cotton lawn or silk dupion are ideal
» Silk chiffon in two shades
» Fringe or tassel trimming
» Quick-dry, clear all-purpose glue
» Bead-headed pins
» Sewing kit

HOW MUCH FABRIC DO I NEED?

To create the pleated effect, you will be pinning strips of chiffon fabric to the frame, pleating as you go. These strips will be a little more than the depth of the shade frame in depth, and approximately one and a half times the bottom (widest) ring circumference in width per colour.

To calculate the width of the fabric strips, first decide how widely-spaced you want the pleats and calculate how many will fit evenly between two vertical struts. For example, on this shade, the distance between two struts is 24cm (9½in) around the bottom ring. So 12 pleats, each 2cm (¹³⁄₁₆in) wide at the bottom will fit nicely. (Naturally these pleats will be closer together around the top ring.) For each pleat, double the spacing width is required in fabric. So the length of the strip of fabric required to pleat around the shade will be: 4cm (1½in) fabric per pleat x 12 pleats per panel x 8 panels per shade = 3.84m (151in) per shade. As two colours are used, just under 2m (2yd) of fabric is required widthways in each colour. It is best to allow a little more than this though, to allow for trimming wastage, so I rounded up to 2m (2yd) per colour.

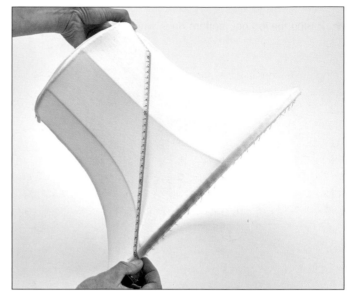

To measure the height of the fabric strips, hold a tape measure at the top ring and bring it around the shade to follow the line of a swathe to the bottom ring. Depending on the shape of the shade, the tape measure is likely to wrap across two or even three panels from top to bottom. Add 8cm (3¼in) for finger pulling room to this measurement. In this case the vertical swathed measurement is 58cm (23in), so I cut my strips 66cm (26¼in) high.

PREPARE YOUR FABRIC

1 Trim off the selvedge from the short ends of the strips (in this case the edge that measures 66cm/26in). Mark the position of the pleats in pencil or soluble fabric pen along the two long edges. As the pleats in this shade each require 4cm (1½in) of fabric, the pencil marks are 4cm (1½in) apart. I chose to have three pleats per stripe of colour, which requires 12cm (4½in) fabric, plus a further 2cm (¹³⁄₁₆in) for overlap at the start and end of each stripe. Cut the strips, as shown.

2 Bind the top and bottom rings with cotton India tape (see pages 22–23). Also bind two vertical struts to create a lining using your lining fabric, using the method described on pages 23–25 and 32. In this case, the lining is fitted to the outside of the frame, not the inside, so your seams will sit on the outside of the frame (2a). This creates a firm base for the chiffon fabric and gives a good finished shape. Once the lining is pinned to a good fit, use lampshade stitch (see page 89) to stitch it to the top and bottom rings. Position the stitches to the front of the rings (2b).

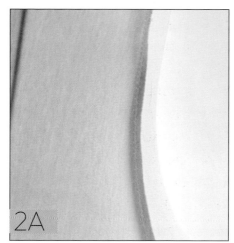
2A

2B

3 Once stitched, trim off the excess fabric evenly. Fold any overlap back over the stitches for a neat finish.

3A

3B

127

4 Mark the position of each pleat with tailor's tacks on the top and bottom rings. These will be pulled out once you've finished, so just one over-stitch should be enough.

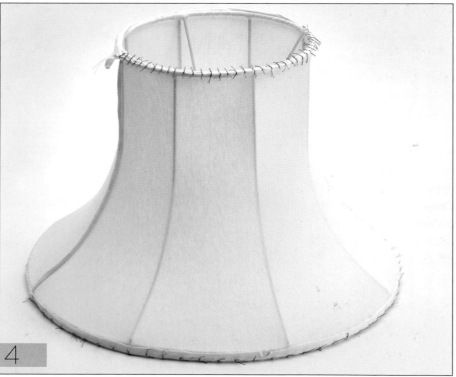
4

▶ **5** Fold the first chiffon strip at the first marker. Pin the fold to the bottom ring at a tailor's tack. Once pinned, bring the folded pleat around and up to the top ring, as far around diagonally as you have planned, and pin to hold the pleat taut and even. At this first fold, aim to have an equal amount of overlap at the top and bottom.

▶ **6** Continue pleating, taking great care to pin at the correct markers, both on the fabric strip and the shade frame. Start by pinning the new fold to the bottom ring first, then the top ring. Aim to keep the chiffon overlap constant at the top and bottom rings. Pin each pleat securely as you work.

▶ **7** The last pleat of the first strip should overlap beyond the fold line of the next pleat. This overlap will be covered by the next pleat, but it is still important to keep the cutting line smooth and straight, as any untidy cutting lines may show through when the light is on. Once you have pinned three pleats, it is time to change to a different colour chiffon.

TIP:

Regularly hold the shade over a light source to check that the pleats are even.

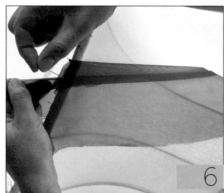

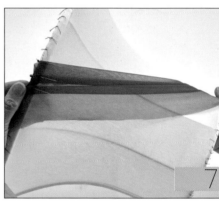

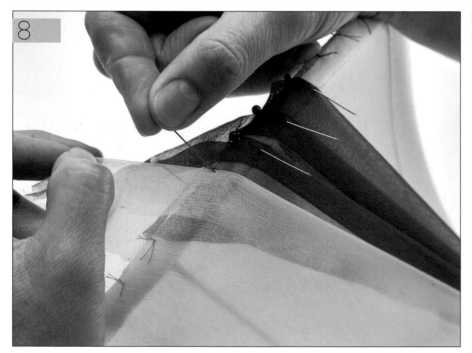

▶ **8** Start the new strip just as you started the first strip.

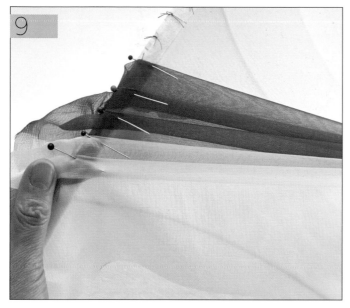

9

9 Continue folding and pinning. Once you have covered one panel in pleated chiffon, it's a good idea to stitch it in place, otherwise you will be overwhelmed by pins and the shade will be tricky to handle.

10 Sew the top ring first. When sewing the bottom ring, pull tension into each pleat, creating a crisper fold. Do not sew the first pleat, but leave it pinned, because it will need to be loose while you fit the last pleat. As you sew the pleats in place, this is a good time to remove each tailor's tack marker, using tweezers or small scissors.

11 Continue pleating strips of coloured chiffon neatly to the shade, stitching finished sections as you work around the shade. Once you have pleated the whole shade frame, the end of the fabric strip should sit behind the first fold. Unpin the first fold and pin the end of the fabric strip to the frame.

TO FINISH

12 Once the top and bottom rings are stitched into place, trim the overlap of chiffon to within 5mm (¼in) of the edge of the rings. Use a very small amount of glue to fold the overlap back over itself, keeping it lying tidy and flat. This edge will be covered with your trimming.

TRIMMING

The trimming for such an ornate shade needs to be considered carefully. Here, a simple tassel trim in the same light shade was chosen, giving all the glory to the chiffon stripes and acknowledging the mid-century era of the shade frame. The braid of the tassel trim is covered in a self-coloured chiffon bias binding, to match the top ring. Of course, you can be as bright and bold as you like. For details on how to add a trim, turn to page 93; see page 69 for making bias binding.

FAUX PLEATS WITH BIAS BINDING

Quick-to-make, smart and sweet, these chic shades are actually covered with bias binding. Bias binding is affordable and plentiful in a vast range of colours – just one roll and you're ready to go. These collar-top shades allow you to create a waistline using ribbon, but the idea works beautifully with bowed empire styles too. These are so quick to make and would be ideal as craft-stall wares or bespoke gifts.

CHOOSING THE RIGHT TAPE

The reason bias binding works so well is that it has some give when pulled. This allows you to wrap the binding evenly and then pull the whole arrangement in further with a waistband for a taut, crisp pleated effect. Bias binding is available in a range of widths. This shade is worked in 25mm (1in) wide binding when folded, which actually opens out to 38mm (1½in). It is more economical to order a whole roll, rather than buy by the metre, as you are likely to use upwards of 20m (22yd) for a medium-sized shade frame.

You will need
- » Collar-top or bowed empire shade frame
- » Cotton India tape
- » A roll of 25mm (1in) bias binding (25m/27yd for small to medium shades, or 50m/55yd for larger shades)
- » Medium- or heavy-weight ribbon: grosgrain or velvet work well
- » Narrow underwear elastic, plain
- » Decorative button (optional)
- » Quick-dry, clear all-purpose glue
- » Sewing kit

130

BINDING YOUR SHADE FRAME

▶ **1** Bind the top and bottom rings of your shade frame in cotton India tape as this will give you a good surface to pin, glue and stitch into (see pages 22–23). To calculate how much the strips will overlap at the top ring, measure the distance between two vertical struts on the top and bottom rings. On these shades, the distance at the bottom is exactly twice that at the top. So, the overlap will be across half the tape at the top, while the binding will sit edge to edge at the bottom. If your shade's top ring is a third of the circumference of the bottom ring, then the overlap will be across two thirds of the tape at the top and the binding will sit edge to edge at the bottom.

▶ **2** Wind your bias binding into a tight roll, leaving a 1m (39in) tail and fasten with a dressmaking pin to prevent it from unrolling. Any longer is likely to tangle while you work. You can let more out by undoing the pin as you go.

▶ **3** Place the shade frame the right way up on the table. Take one end of the bias binding. Holding it with right side facing you, open up the right-hand fold. Pin the end to the inside of the top ring, just to the right of a vertical strut. Do not glue as you will need to tuck the last strip underneath this strip to finish.

▶ **4** Bring the binding down the front of the frame and loop under the bottom ring, again lining up the left-hand side of the tape with the vertical strut.

▶ **5** Bring the binding back up the inside of the shade frame and over the top ring, overlapping, in this case, half of the previous bias-binding strip.

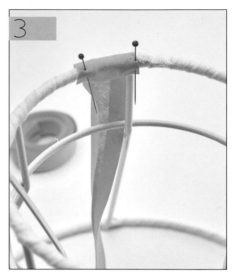

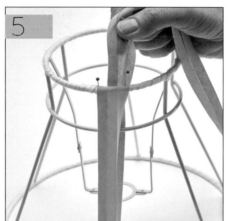

▶ **6** Bring the tape back down to the bottom and this time overlap the tape over the right-hand fold, so that the front face of the bias binding strips are edge to edge.

▶ **7** Continue in this way around the shade. The binding tape should line up with each vertical strut as it did at the start. Check each time you reach one that all is correct.

STARTING A NEW LENGTH

▶ **8** Finish the length at the top or bottom ring, and glue the end neatly to the inside of the ring, then pin taut (8a). Trim off the excess (8b). Take a new length, open out the right-hand side flap, fold the end over and glue this fold in line with the previous length. Pin into place to hold while the glue sets and continue binding (8c).

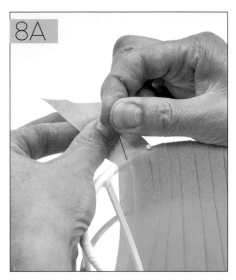

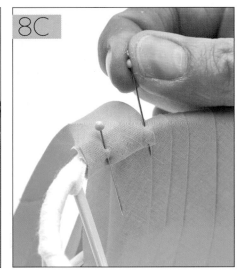

NAVIGATING GIMBALS

You will have to make some discreet snips to navigate the gimbal fittings inside the shade.

▶ **9** When the binding reaches a gimbal, snip sideways into the tape, from left to right, just past the gimbal fitting (9a). Tuck this overlap behind the gimbal fitting (9b). You may have to do this twice in a row. Once past the gimbal fitting, the binding should neatly cover these snipped lengths (9c).

ENDING NEATLY

▶ **10** When you have finished binding, finish off at the top or bottom ring on the inside. Fold over the end and glue discreetly to the ring. You may need to tuck the binding under the first length for a perfectly invisible finish.

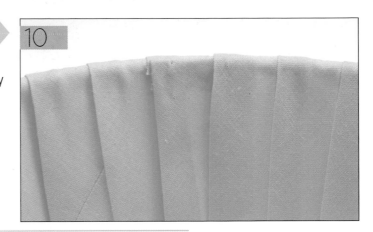

FITTING THE RIBBON WAISTBAND

The ribbon waistband fits around the narrowest girth of the shade, in this case around the collar.

▶ **11** To start, place your wrapped shade on the table. Cut a length of narrow underwear elastic and tie it around the waist of the shade. Pull in tightly enough to draw the bias binding in snugly around the waist. Knot neatly and trim the ends. This elastic will stay in place underneath the ribbon. Tie a length of decorative ribbon around the waist, covering the elastic. Stitch in place with a few stitches in matching thread.

KNOTS AND BOWS

▶ **12** Cover the join in the ribbon with a quirky knot, tidy bow or even a button. Keep it simple and unfussy.

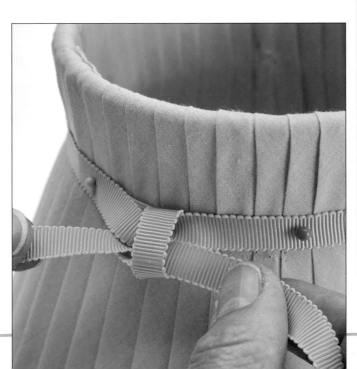

PARTY SHADES

Imagine a garden party festooned with beautiful lampshades dangling from branches or cascading in bunches at the marquee entrance… These fabulously colourful and quick-to-make organza ribbon lampshades are the perfect project. Each one takes just minutes to make and can be lit with a simple LED battery light, so no pesky trailing wires either. Party time!

136

CHOOSING THE RIGHT RIBBON

Organza ribbon is transparent, sheeny, available in dozens of colours and widths and, when bought in large quantities, very affordable. That makes it an ideal choice for this project. The idea is to make several lampshades in little time. You will achieve a pleated look by overlapping layers of ribbon bound around the frame. On close inspection, they will not be as refined as traditional pleated shades, but will look fabulous festooned together. One safety note: organza ribbon is usually made from synthetic fibres, so is not appropriate for lighting with standard domestic light bulbs. Small battery-powered LED lights are ideal, as they give off no heat and will require no trailing wires.

You will need

» A selection of collar-top or bowed empire shade frames in mixed sizes
» Rolls of 25mm (1in) organza ribbon in various colours
» Sewing kit
» Quick-dry, clear all-purpose glue
» LED battery lights

TIP:

A good alternative to ribbon would be to cut strips of transparent organza fabric.

PREPARING YOUR SHADE FRAME

There is no need to bind the shade frame first.

▶ **1** To calculate how much the strips will overlap at the top ring, measure the distance between the vertical struts on the top and bottom rings. On most shades, the distance at the bottom is up to twice that at the top. So, if your shade's top ring is half that of the bottom ring, the overlap will be across half the tape at the top, and the ribbon will sit edge to edge at the bottom. If your shade's top ring is a third of the circumference of the bottom ring, then the overlap will be across two thirds of the tape at the top and the ribbon will sit edge to edge at the bottom.

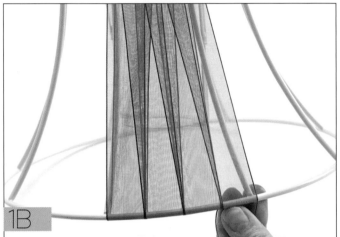

At the top ring the ribbon overlaps halfway.
At the bottom ring the ribbon sits edge to edge.

BINDING YOUR SHADE FRAME

▶ **2** Wind your length of ribbon into a tight roll, leaving a 1m (39in) tail and fasten with a dressmaking pin to prevent it from unrolling. Any longer is likely to tangle while you work. You can let more out by undoing the pin as you go.

▶ **3** Place the shade frame the right way up on the table. Take the end of the ribbon and hold onto the inside of the top ring, just to the right of a vertical strut. Pin. Do not glue at this stage as you will need to tuck the last strip underneath this strip to finish.

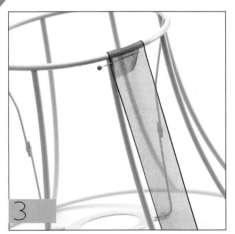

▶ **4** Bring the ribbon down the front of the frame and loop under the bottom ring, lining up the left-hand side of the ribbon with the vertical strut.

▶ **5** Bring the ribbon back up the inside of the shade frame and over the top ring, overlapping a portion of the previous strip. If you find it helpful, pin to hold the two overlapping layers in place, enabling you to let go of the end.

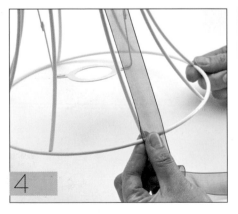
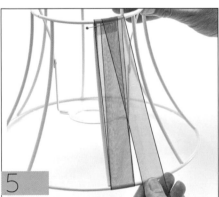

6 Bring the ribbon back down to the bottom and butt up the edges, so that the ribbon strips are edge to edge at the bottom ring.

7 Continue in this way around the shade. The ribbon should line up with each vertical strut as it did at the start. Check each time you reach a strut that all is correct.

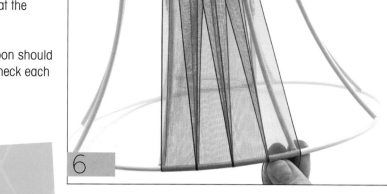

6

TIP: *If you find that the ribbon slips about while you work, try adhering a narrow strip of double sided tape around the inside of the top and bottom rings.*

NAVIGATING GIMBALS

As on the previous lampshade (see page 130), you will have to make some discreet snips to navigate the gimbals inside the shade.

8 When the ribbon reaches a gimbal, snip sideways into it, from left to right, just past the gimbal fitting (8a). Tuck this overlap behind the gimbal fitting (8b). You may have to do this twice in a row. Once past the gimbal fitting, the ribbon should neatly cover these snipped areas (8c).

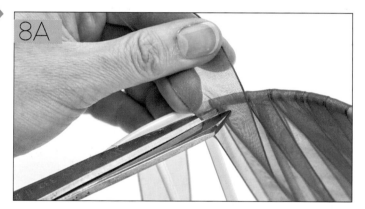

8A

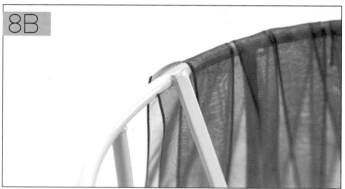

8B

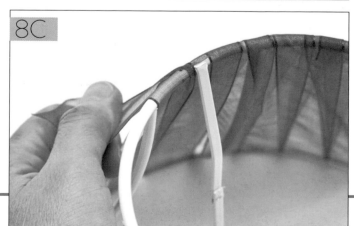

8C

STARTING A NEW LENGTH

▶ **9** Finish the length at the top or bottom ring, and trim (this is to ensure that the seam you are about to sew is hidden by the ring. Take a new length of ribbon and stitch the two ends together using a matching thread. Simply continue wrapping the shade as before.

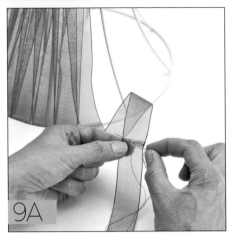

9A

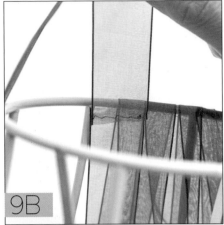

9B

ENDING NEATLY

▶ **10** When you have finished wrapping, finish off at the bottom ring on the inside. Fold over the end and glue discreetly to the bottom ring. You may need to tuck the ribbon behind the first length for an almost invisible finish.

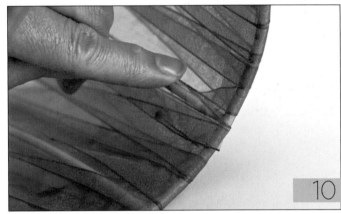

10

FITTING THE RIBBON WAISTBAND

The ribbon waistband fits around the narrowest girth of the shade, in this case around the collar.

▶ **11** To start, place your wrapped shade on the table. Cut a length of ribbon – either matching or contrasting – and pin the centre of it to the back of the shade (11a). Wrap round the shade and pull in tightly to draw the ribbon in snugly around the waist. Tie neatly in a bow (11b).

▶ **12** To give the ends of your ribbon a professional finish, fold them in half then snip diagonally, as shown.

11A

11B

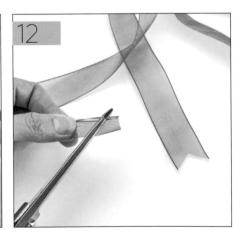

12

Loose projects

REVERSIBLE KITCHEN SHADE

These removable, washable lampshade covers are ideal for a busy, action-packed family room. And, because they are reversible, you have two looks to choose from. How about summer and winter versions? These simple semi-loose covers can be made to fit anything from teeny wall lights and chandelier shades to standard-lamp frames. The pretty covers are simply a tube of fabric elasticated at both ends, nipped in with a smart ribbon at the waist: easy, simple to make and practical. These have been made for a set of cute cottage-loaf frames, but the idea works beautifully with bowed empire and collar-top frames too.

CHOOSING THE RIGHT FABRIC

Each cover is made with two layers of fabric, so fine fabrics are ideal, especially on smaller shades. Cotton lawns, patchworking cottons and lightweight linens all work well, especially if you intend to wash them regularly. Bear in mind that when the lights are on, colour and pattern on the reverse side will show through.

HOW MUCH FABRIC DO I NEED?

For each shade, your top and lining fabric pieces will measure approximately 3cm (1¼in) wider than the circumference of the shade at its widest point, and approximately 2.5cm (1in) deeper than the length of one of the vertical struts. These cottage-loaf frames measure 42cm (16½in) around their widest point. So, the width of each piece of fabric is 45cm (17¾in) – the circumference plus 3cm (1¼in) for turnings.

Each vertical strut measures 13cm (5in): note that this is NOT the height of the shade but the actual length of each strut. The depth of each fabric piece is therefore 15.5cm (6in) – the height of the strut plus 2.5cm/1in extra for gathers and turnings.

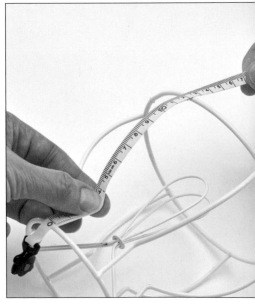

PREPARING YOUR SHADE FRAME

On this style of shade, the cover slips over the bare frame. No binding is required.

SEWING YOUR FABRIC COVERS

▶ **1** For each shade, fold each strip of top cover and lining fabric in half right sides together and pin along the short seam, ready for machine sewing.

▶ **2** For each piece, sew along the pinned seam, 1cm (⅜in) from the raw edge. Press the seam open, and leave inside out. Repeat for the lining fabrics but turn right side out.

▶ **3** Pair up the top covers with the linings. Tuck a lining inside a top cover, so that the right sides are facing, lining up the seams. Pin around the top edge. Sew this top edge, 5mm (¼in) from the top edge. Trim away any loose threads or frayed ends.

▶ **4** Turn the right way out and press so that the top sewn seam is crisp and neat. Sew a second line approximately 1cm (⅜in) below the top sewn edge. This will be the channel that houses the top elastic drawstring.

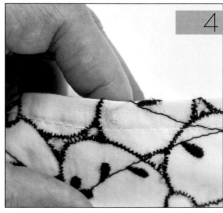

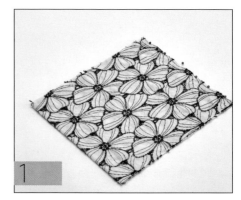

▶ **5** Now turn the two bottom edges under, by approximately 5mm (¼in), and pin. Machine sew these two turned-under edges together, keeping your sewing line as close to the edge as possible. Press to give a crisp turned edge. Now machine sew a second line approximately 1cm (⅜in) from the first sewn line. This will house the elastic around the bottom edge.

SLOTTING IN THE ELASTIC

▶ **6** Cut a piece of elastic the length of the circumference of the bottom ring. Fasten a safety pin to one end. The safety pin must be narrower than the sewn channels. Snip open the stitches at the seam, within the sewn channel. This is likely to be just two or three stitches. Take care not to snip too many.

▶ **7** Slot the safety pin into the hole and push around the sewn channel, easing the fabric across the elastic as you go. Push out at the other end.

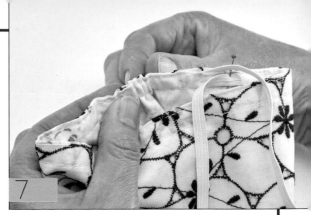

▶ **8** Arrange the fabric gathers evenly around the elastic. The length of the elastic should be narrower than the ring of the shade, so that it pulls the fabric taut around the ring yet has enough give to allow the cover to be slipped on to the shade. Sew the two ends together firmly and trim the ends.

▶ **9** Ease the excess elastic into the channel and slip stitch the opening closed. Repeat for the top ring, taking a new elastic measurement. Your cover is now ready to fit onto the shade frame.

FITTING THE COVER

▶ **10** Carefully pull the cover over the shade frame, from the top. Arrange the gathers evenly and ensure the top and bottom openings are nicely centred.

▶ **11** Before fitting the ribbon in place, tie a length of elastic around the waist of the shade to pull in the shape; trim off the excess elastic. Arrange the fabric and gathers evenly.

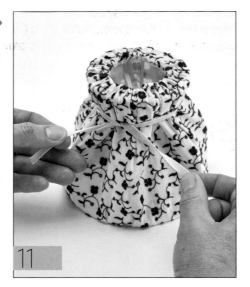

▶ **12** Cut a length of ribbon long enough to span the narrow waist of the shade, plus enough overlap to fit. Attach the buckle with a few neat stitches, wrap around the shade and fasten. Now your shade is ready to use.

WASHING TIPS:

* Many fabrics shrink when washed the first time. Check for pre-shrinkage or wash before making up the shades.
* Wash and press while a little damp to get rid of stubborn creases.
* If using two strongly coloured fabrics, check the dyes will not run before using.
* Many ribbons do not wash well. It may be best to fit a new ribbon after washing for a crisp fresh look.

EASY LOOSE COVER

Quick-to-make loose covers can revive any size of hard-sided drum or cone shade. Smart and practical, they are made from washable cotton fabric. A contrasting lining makes them reversible too. If you are considering a new decorating scheme, these could be just the answer...

CHOOSING THE RIGHT FABRIC

Each cover is made with two layers of fabric, so fine fabrics are ideal, especially on smaller shades. Cotton lawns, patchworking cottons and lightweight linens all work well, especially if you intend to wash them regularly. Bear in mind that when the light is on, colour and pattern on the reverse side will show through.

You will need

» A hard-sided cone shade in need of recovering
» Top and lining fabrics: washable cotton and linens are ideal
» Medium-weight washable ribbon
» Pattern paper or old sheeting
» Sewing kit

CREATING YOUR TEMPLATE

For each shade, your top and lining fabric pieces will measure the same size as the cone shade they are to cover, with a little extra for depth and turnings. This makes them very economical in fabric.

▷ **1** First, wrap the cone shade in a piece of paper or old calico or sheeting. Pin into place and use a soft pencil or fabric marker to mark the top and bottom rings and the overlapping line, which should be vertical. Remove from the shade and trim to size, allowing a 2.5cm (1in) overlap. Re-check the fit.

1

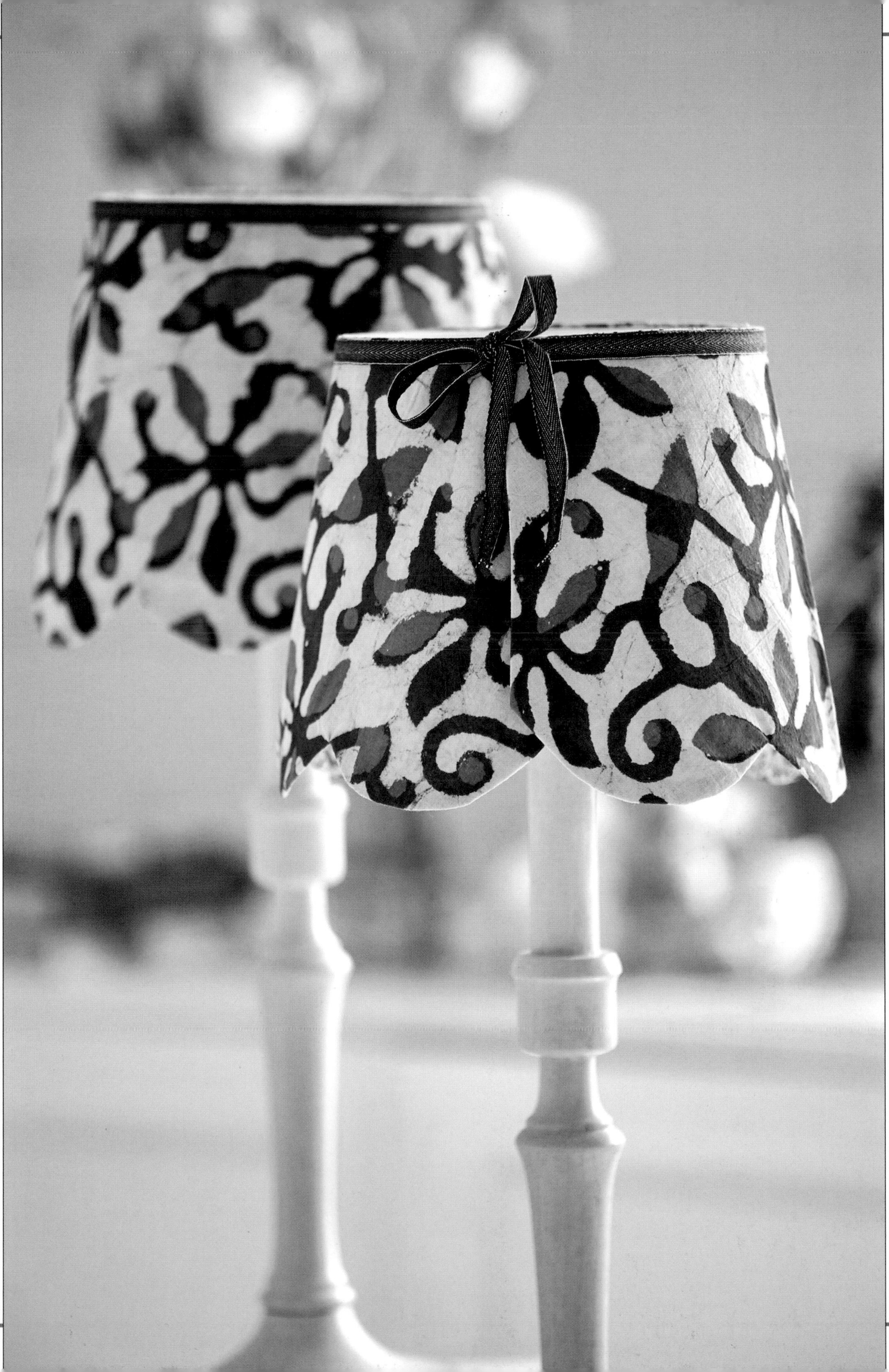

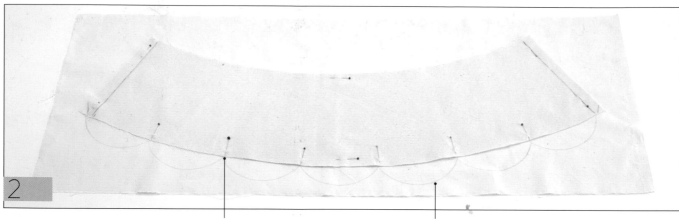

2 To create the scallops, lay your template flat and mark out a 2.5cm (1in) overlap at each end. In between the overlaps, position pins evenly along the bottom edge – each pin indicates the width of a scallop. I find that seven is a good number for a medium-sized lampshade.

3 Place the pinned template onto another piece of paper or sheeting fabric. Using a compass, or drawing around a cup or bowl, mark even scallops onto the bottom edge to create a new scalloped template, using the pins as a guide. Note how the two end scallops continue up to the side edges.

4 Cut out this new template. This is the one you will use to cut out your top and lining fabrics.

PREPARING YOUR FABRIC

5 Lay your top and lining fabrics right sides together on the worktable. Position and pin the template on top. Note that the template indicates the sewing line, so you will need to allow at least 1.5cm (⅝in) seam allowance around all sides; cut out the fabrics.

6 Use contrasting thread to tack/baste a running stitch line around the edge of the template. You will follow this line with your sewing machine.

7 Use matching thread to machine sew along the tacking/basting line. You will need to leave a 15cm (6in) gap at the top edge to allow for turning out. Once sewn, trim the seam allowance to 1cm (⅜in) neatly around all sides.

TRIMMING AND TURNING OUT

▶ **8** In order for the fabric to lie flat and the indent of each scallop not to be puckered, you must cut notches at intervals around the curves of each scallop. Make sure there is a notch right in the indent. It will help to trim bulk from each corner too.

▶ **9** Turn out the sewn cover through the gap in the top edge. Carefully push the seam right to the edge at each scallop and indent. It may help to tweak with a pin to get the sewn line right to the edge. Now press.

FINISHING

A length of washable ribbon is by far the easiest way of fastening the loose cover, and adds an informal decorative finish to the top edge.

▶ **10** Before you add the ribbon, slip stitch the turning gap closed, and press.

▶ **11** Pin a length of ribbon along the top edge, leaving ends of about 25cm (10in). Hand or machine sew the ribbon in place, leaving one end unsewn by 2.5cm (1in) to allow for the overlap.

▶ **12** Wrap your old shade in its new cover, and tie the ribbon in a bow.

Trimmings

Making your own trimmings is the way to achieve truly bespoke lampshades. Here are six of the most useful handmade decorative edges, created by simply pleating and gathering fabrics. Be bold with proportions, have fun with colour combinations, and mix and match fabrics and ribbons to make your handmade lampshades really stand out.

CHOOSING THE RIGHT FABRICS

Understanding how fabric behaves when pressed, pleated, gathered or ruched is vital to getting the right effect when making a trimming. For example, the centrally gathered trim on shade A, right, is made using a tube of silk chiffon, a very light, soft and floppy fabric, which rolls voluptuously when gathered. The same centrally gathered trim on shade B, right, is made using much stiffer silk dupion, doubled up and left with a raw edge cut with pinking shears. The fabric stands out more stiffly, creating crisper folds and edges, and the many-coloured sheen creates even more complexity – a proper ruffle! I would advise you to experiment with different fabrics, to see what effects you like.

TRIMMING CONSIDERATIONS

- For most styles of handmade trim, the fabric strip will be two to three times longer than the circumference of the frame ring. For a larger shade this will require a join, which is best done diagonally to make it less noticeable (see page 46). As each strip may be 5–10cm (2–4in) in depth, trimmings can use up a lot of fabric, in some cases more than the amount required to cover the shade.
- A wealth of fabulous ribbon is available for crafters. Its benefit to lampshade makers is that it usually has a woven selvedge, so there is no need for bulky turnings. Satins, gauzy weaves, stripes, checks and spots can look fabulous when pleated and gathered. You can even try combining ribbons.
- The size of the shade will determine the proportion of the trimming. The shades on the next few pages are all just 12cm (4¾in) high, and on average the strips used to make up the trimmings were 5cm (2in), two-fifths of the height. They are large for maximum impact, but bear in mind that meanly proportioned trimmings rarely look great. I would advise that you work out the proportion of your trimming using a scrap of old sheeting before you begin.
- Glue or stitching? Applying the trimming with glue allows you to achieve a neat straight edge quickly. I apply a fine line of glue to the edge of the shade, then press the trimming onto it, pinning as I work. When the glue is set, a few hand stitches through the trimming help secure it in place and prevent it from accidentally being pulled away by curious fingers.

6 HANDMADE TRIMS

1. GATHERED FRILL

▶ **1** Cut a strip of fabric or ribbon three times the circumference of the ring.

▶ **2** Hand sew a row of small running stitches in strong thread along the top edge of the strip, approximately 3mm (⅛in) in from the edge.

▶ **3** Draw the running stitches up to gather the strip to the required length and sew to knot off.

▶ **4** Glue or stitch the frill to the shade, turning the ends under and making sure they butt up to create an invisible join.

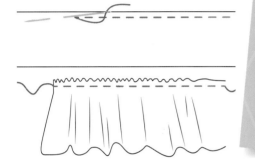

TIP:
For a deep frill, two rows of hand stitches 1mm apart help prevent the frill from twisting while you apply it to the shade.

Cheery 4cm (1½in) gingham ribbon gathered at the top edge.

2. PLEATED FRILL

▶ **1** Cut a strip of ribbon or fabric three times the circumference of the ring. In this case, two ribbons were layered together.

▶ **2** For finished pleats that are 2cm (¹³⁄₁₆in) wide, position a pin every 2cm (¹³⁄₁₆in) along the length of the ribbon. Use these pins as a guide to work along the length folding each pleat. Re-pin the pleats into place, taking care to keep the folds straight.

▶ **3** Hand tack/baste the pleats into position with at least two rows of running stitches along the top and bottom edges, catching each pleat into place. Remove the pins and press the pleats firmly.

▶ **4** Machine sew one or two rows of stitches 2mm (¹⁄₁₆in) apart along the top edge. Press again before removing the tacking/basting stitches.

▶ **5** Glue or stitch the pleated frill to the underside of the shade, making sure the two ends overlap neatly to create a discreet join.

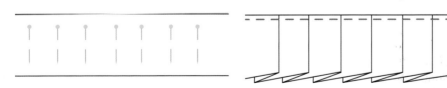

The scalloped edge allows the frill to kick out like a skirt.

3. CENTRE-GATHERED FRILL

▶ **1** Cut a strip of fabric three times the circumference of the ring. In this case, two strips were doubled up. Use pinking shears if desired.

▶ **2** Use strong thread to hand sew a row of small running stitches along the centre of the strip. Aim to keep the visible stitch on the front of the strip as small as you can.

▶ **3** Draw the running stitches up to gather the strip to the required length and sew to knot off.

▶ **4** Glue or stitch to the shade with the centre stitch line sitting on the edge of the shade; turn the ends under and make sure they butt up to create an invisible join.

 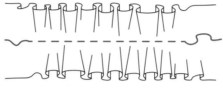

Two strips of silk fabric cut with pinking shears are doubled up for an extravagant ruffle.

4. BOX-PLEATED FRILL

▶ **1** Cut a strip of ribbon three times the circumference of the ring.

▶ **2** The ideal width of each box pleat is the width of the strip, which makes a square box pleat. Use pins to measure each fold along the length, alternating a full width and a half width.

▶ **3** Now use these positional pins to fold and re-pin the ribbon, folding in different directions each time to create the box pleats. When pinning, take care that each fold is straight.

▶ **4** Hand tack/baste into position with at least two rows of running stitches along the top and bottom edges, catching each pleat into place. Press the pleats firmly.

▶ **5** Machine sew along the top edge of the folded strip, then a second line 2mm (1/16 in) below it. Remove the tacking/basting stitches and press again.

▶ **6** Glue or stitch to the shade, making sure the two ends overlap neatly to create a discreet join. Here, I covered the raw top edge of the box-pleated ribbon with a slim length of velvet ribbon.

Fabulous box-pleated polka dot ribbon.

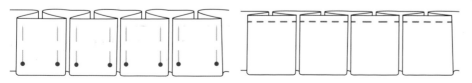

5. BUTTERFLY-PLEATED FRILL

▶ **1** Follow the instructions for making a box pleat (see facing page) steps 1–4.

▶ **2** Machine sew along the centre of the strip, taking care that the pleats lie flat as you sew. Remove the tacking/basting and press again.

▶ **3** Bring the centre point of the top and bottom of each pleat towards the middle stitched line and hand sew in place.

▶ **4** Glue or stitch the trimming to the shade, sitting the centre stitched line of the frill on the edge of the shade. End with two folds butting together for a discreet join.

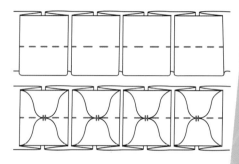

Taking box pleats a stage further to create a formal structural trim.

TIP:
When sewing the centre line, a decorative strip of braid can be attached at the same time. Similarly, beads or other decorative embellishments can be attached to the centres of each fold.

6. PETAL RUFFLE

▶ **1** Cut a strip of ribbon or fabric three times the circumference of the ring.

▶ **2** Position pins along the length, spaced the same distance apart as the width of the strip.

▶ **3** Use strong matching sewing thread to hand sew a zigzag line of running stitch along the strip, using the pins as guides. Remove the pins as you go.

▶ **4** Draw the running stitches up to gather the strip to the required length and sew to knot off.

▶ **5** Turn the ends under then glue or stitch the trim to the shade, making sure the two ends butt up to create an invisible join. (See also page 48.)

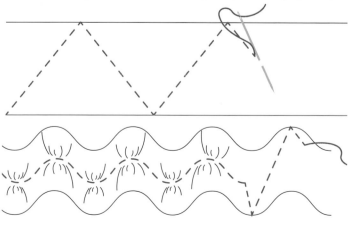

Wide crinkly taffeta ribbon creates beautifully crisp informal scallops.

Ideas for stands

For a conventional look, the width of the bottom ring should be around four-fifths of the height of the base.

Consider the size of the base in relation to the height of the shade. A common 'rule' is that the shade should be about a third of the total height... but in this case, where the stand is so wide, I decided the height proportions should be closer to 50:50.

Here, the width of the shade is about the height of the stand.

There are no hard-and-fast rules about the proportion of the shade to the base – often it is just whether you feel it looks right in the setting. If you are struggling to decide, it often helps to cut out a paper shape of a shade and hold it up to the base to see how well it works visually; you could try doing the same with a paper cut-out of a base. However, there are a few basic principles which may be helpful when deciding.

If the shade is more than twice the height of the base, it may look top-heavy; but this may be a look you want.

Lamp stands are available in a huge range of styles. They can also be found cheaply in charity shops and auctions, and freshened up with paint. Always remember to have a second-hand lamp base safety-tested by an electrician.

The shape and size of the lampshade should complement the room, and also the base. A good design principle is to team an ornate shade with a plain base, and vice versa. If the base and shade are the same colour, keep the shapes fairly simple.

Index